"A clearly written account of a centrally important issue—the influence (or not) of ancient Near Eastern thought upon Old Testament writers. John Currid's books and commentaries have proven invaluable, and in this additional volume, his thorough research, theological acumen, and nuanced argumentation makes it an essential requirement for ministers, theological students, and serious students of Scripture. This is an invaluable aid in furthering our understanding of the Old Testament and a loud affirmation of the Bible's utter trustworthiness and inerrancy. A marvelous book."

> **Derek Thomas,** Minister of Preaching and Teaching, First Presbyterian Church, Columbia, South Carolina; Professor of Systematic Theology and Historical Theology, Reformed Theological Seminary, Atlanta

"This is a splendid introduction to the use that the Old Testament makes of the religious ideas of Israel's ancient neighbors. Currid compares the biblical accounts of creation and the flood with the versions from neighboring cultures and shows how the Bible puts down and rejects the theological ideas of Babylon, Egypt, the Hittites, and the Canaanites. This process, which Currid terms 'polemical theology', serves to demonstrate the unique sovereignty of the God of Israel. This is a very positive approach to the issues raised by the extrabiblical parallels and is greatly preferable to seeing the parallels as showing the Bible as simply borrowed pagan ideas and myths."

> **Gordon J. Wenham,** Adjunct Professor, Old Testament, Trinity College, Bristol, England

"In this vital work John Currid presents an enormously useful approach to understanding the relationship of the Old Testament to the literature and thought of Israel's ancient Near Eastern neighbors. This book is certainly a must read for any Old Testament scholar, yet it also provides a relevant and readable introduction for every student of Scripture."

> **David W. Chapman,** Professor of New Testament and Archaeology, Covenant Theological Seminary; author, *Ancient Jewish and Christian Perceptions of Crucifixion*

"A rising influential voice in Old Testament studies is asserting that the biblical worldview, while monotheistic, often parallels and at times pirates with minimal discrimination the pre-enlightened religious ideas and rituals of ancient Israel's neighbors. In contrast, John Currid persuasively demonstrates in *Against the Gods* that the Bible's tendency is not to appropriate but to dispute and repudiate pagan myths, ideas, identities, and customs. This important introduction to Old Testament polemical theology provides a balanced corrective to many current comparative studies."

> **Jason S. DeRouchie,** Associate Professor of Old Testament, Bethlehem College and Seminary

"If you're like me, you need to know a lot more about biblical backgrounds and how to think about them. John Currid's *Against the Gods* is a great place to start."

James M. Hamilton, Associate Professor of Biblical Theology, The Southern Baptist Theological Seminary; author, *God's Glory in Salvation through Judgment*

Against the Gods

AGAINST
THE
GODS

THE POLEMICAL THEOLOGY OF THE OLD TESTAMENT

JOHN D. CURRID

WHEATON, ILLINOIS

Trade paperback ISBN: 978-1-4335-3183-5
ePub ISBN: 978-1-4335-3186-6
PDF ISBN: 978-1-4335-3184-2
Mobipocket ISBN: 978-1-4335-3185-9

Library of Congress Cataloging-in-Publication Data

Currid, John D., 1951-
  Against the gods : the polemical theology of the Old Testament / John D. Currid.
      pages cm
  Includes bibliographical references and index.
  ISBN 978-1-4335-3183-5
  1. Bible. O.T.—Criticism, interpretation, etc. 2. Middle Eastern literature—History and criticism. 3. Polemics—Religious aspects. I. Title.
BS1171.3.C87   2013
221.6—dc23   2013004991

Contents

Prologue

This book is about the relationship between the writings of the Old Testament and other ancient Near Eastern literature. It is a difficult, complicated, and much-debated topic in the field of biblical studies today. To be frank, there is little consensus regarding exactly how the two relate to each other. There are extremes, to be sure: on the one hand, some believe that ancient Near Eastern studies have little to contribute to our understanding of the Old Testament and, in fact, constitute a danger to Scripture. On the other hand, there are some who would say that the Old Testament is not unique but it is merely another expression of ancient Near Eastern literature that is grounded in myth, legend, and folklore. Surely the truth lies somewhere between the two extremes. It is certainly undeniable that the historical, geographical, and cultural context of the Bible is the ancient Near East, and study of the era has much to add to our understanding of the Old Testament. But it is also true that the Old Testament worldview is unique in the ancient Near East, and this is immediately confirmed by its all-pervasive monotheism. It simply does not swallow ancient Near Eastern thought hook, line, and sinker. And so, the question for modern minds in this regard is, what precisely is the relationship of the Old Testament to ancient Near Eastern literature?

This book attempts to look at one particular slice of this large and multifaceted issue. My hope is to advance the debate a little, stir up some thoughts, and perhaps make some progress in the discussion. The book, however, is not written for scholars, although I hope some scholars may benefit from it. The work is *introductory* and, therefore, is designed for those who know little about the topic of polemical theology. My desire is that it might invigorate people to do further study in the Old Testament and its relationship with ancient Near Eastern culture and thought.

The study is also meant to be *exemplary* and not exhaustive. In other words, I do not consider every case of polemical theology in the Old Testament, nor is every example I consider done in exhaustive detail. My objective is to demonstrate that the concept of polemics is not foreign to or uncommon in the Old Testament. And, in fact, polemical writing was commonly practiced throughout the entire ancient Near East.[1]

The study is also not meant to be *reductionistic*. The relationship between the Old Testament and ancient Near Eastern literature and culture is quite complex. I am focusing on only one aspect of that relationship, and it is obviously only one lens by which to look at the material. There are numerous other lenses that ought to be employed to examine the material in order to arrive at a fully developed perspective on this vast issue. I am aware that I may be accused of being *minimalistic*, but that is certainly not my intention. My desire is to push things forward in order to stimulate conversation.

The main ideas of the monograph were originally presented in a series of lectures I gave at the Fall Conference at Reformed Theological Seminary–Charlotte in 2007. That three-part series was entitled, "Crass Plagiarism: The Problem of the Relationship of the Old Testament to Ancient Near Eastern Literature." Much has been added to that seminal work, and this new material has been included in this book. In many ways, it remains a work in process, and I hope to write on the topic for years to come.

It is a pleasure to take a moment to thank those who helped in the preparation of this manuscript. First, I would like to thank my teaching assistant, Lacy Larson, for her labors in this project. I am grateful, as well, to Reformed Theological Seminary–Charlotte for granting me a study leave to produce the book. Justin Taylor of Crossway was encouraging to me from beginning to end, and I appreciate his support of this project.

---

[1] See, for example, John D. Currid, *Ancient Egypt and the Old Testament* (Grand Rapids, MI: Baker, 1997), page 62 and note 64.

1

A Brief History of Ancient Near Eastern Studies

Ancient Near Eastern study today is a highly developed discipline that includes much modern technology, with computer analysis and data organization as dominating forces. Obviously, this has not always been the case because at its inception in the beginning of the nineteenth century no such tools were available. As we will see, the first researchers in the discipline were those who discovered unknown languages and those who deciphered them. In reality, the serious examination and study of the cultures of the ancient Near East are relatively recent phenomena. The field of study is barely two hundred years old. Presently, the discipline is thriving, becoming specialized, and the amount of information is exploding.[1] How did such a development occur in a mere two-hundred-year period? How did the discipline evolve into what it is today? This chapter will attempt to do two things: first, it will provide a cursory outline of the history of ancient Near Eastern studies and, second, it will briefly consider the relationship of that field to the field of biblical studies.

---

[1] One example of specialization is that my terminal degree is a PhD in Syro-Palestinian Archaeology in the Department of Near Eastern Languages and Civilizations at the University of Chicago. Many people that I give that information to have absolutely no idea what I am talking about!

The Beginnings of Research in the Ancient Near East (1798–1872)

Prior to 1798, the world's knowledge of the history of the ancient Near East was principally derived from the Bible and from some early Greek writers who preserved some aspects of it in their own histories. One of the more important of these historians was Herodotus, who lived in the fifth century BC. He introduced his history with a famous statement:

> I, Herodotus of Halicarnassus, am here setting forth my history, that time may not draw the color from what man has brought into being, nor those great and wonderful deeds, manifested by both Greeks and barbarians, fail of their report, and, together with all this, the reason why they fought one another.[2]

One of Herodotus's primary goals in writing a history was to give explanation and understanding to the hostilities between the Greeks and the Persians that occurred in the first half of the fifth century BC. Part of his work included some information about the histories of Egypt, Babylon, Assyria, Phoenicia, and other areas of the ancient Near East. Much of his testimony came from oral tradition that was provided by contemporary natives of the fifth century BC, such as the priests of Egypt. The trustworthiness of Herodotus's history is a matter of raging debate: to some he is "the father of history," and to others he is "the father of lies." [3] No matter, the evidence of the history of the ancient Near East prior to the nineteenth century was paltry.

Archaeology was of little help before the nineteenth century in providing evidence for our understanding of the ancient Near East. The field of archaeology was in existence before that century; modern fieldwork had begun with organized digs at Herculaneum, located on the Bay of Naples, in AD 1738:[4]

> Tunnels dug at Herculaneum led to the recovery of magnificent statuary now housed in the Naples Museum. Karl Weber drew some very ac-

---

[2] David Grene, trans., *The History of Herodotus* (Chicago: University of Chicago Press, 1987), 33.
[3] A. R. Burn, *Herodotus: The Histories* (Baltimore: Penguin, 1954), 13.
[4] William F. Albright, *From the Stone Age to Christianity*, 2nd ed. (Garden City, NY: Doubleday, 1957), 26.

curate architectural plans during these early excavations. The digs were eventually suspended at Herculaneum because of the great problem of having to chop through meters of volcanic residue that covered the site.[5]

Excavations at Pompeii soon followed, beginning in 1748. The first buildings to be excavated included "the smaller theatre (or Odeon, 1764), the Temple of Isis (1764), the so-called Gladiator's barracks (1767), and the Villa of Diomedes outside the Herculaneum Gate (1771)."[6] Systematic archaeological work in the Near East, however, did not begin until the turn into the nineteenth century. The first great stride in the field was in Egyptian research. In 1798 Napoleon invaded Egypt. He brought with him a scientific expedition of scholars, architects, and draftsmen whose primary purpose was to survey the ancient monuments of Egypt. The account of their findings was published in a series of tomes, from 1809–1829, titled *Description de l'Egypte*.[7] This exploration was important because Egypt was the first ancient land of the Near East rediscovered in modern times: it opened up the eyes of the West to a vast ancient civilization. When Napoleon's army gathered at the base of the pyramids to engage the Mameluke army in battle (July 21, 1798), Napoleon said to his troops, "Soldiers! From atop these pyramids, fifty centuries look down upon you!" This message was not merely encouragement for the French expeditionary force; it was intended for all Europe.

In regard to the future of Egyptian archaeology, Napoleon's expedition made a most important discovery: the Valley of the Kings.[8] From the Eighteenth–Twentieth Dynasties, which is the New Kingdom period of Egyptian history (c. 1550–1070 BC), the Egyptian rulers at Thebes built for themselves royal tombs on the west side of the Nile River.[9] The Valley of the Kings contains more than sixty tombs, although not all of them be-

---

[5] John D. Currid, *Doing Archaeology in the Land of the Bible* (Grand Rapids, MI: Baker, 1999), 18.
[6] E. Gersbach, "Herculaneum and Pompeii," in *The Oxford Companion to Archaeology*, ed. Brian Fagan (New York: Oxford University Press, 1996), 274–275.
[7] To view the copperplate engravings produced by the expedition, see Gilles Neret, *Description de l'Egypte* (Berlin: Taschen, 2007).
[8] The first to identify the site was the Jesuit Claude Sicard (1677–1726), but he did no archaeological work in the area. See John Baines and Jaromir Malek, *Atlas of Ancient Egypt* (New York: Facts on File, 1980), 24.
[9] The New Kingdom in Egypt is the time period in which many scholars would date the Hebrew exodus out of Egypt.

long to royalty. This area, of course, became a central spot for excavation work beginning in the middle of the nineteenth century and continuing today. The most famous discovery here was the tomb of Pharaoh Tutankhamen by the archaeologist Howard Carter in 1922.

The reality is that no real advances could be made until the hieroglyphic language was deciphered, which leads us to consider the most significant find of the Napoleonic excursion: the Rosetta Stone (1799):

> It proved to be invaluable because it was the key to unlocking ancient Egyptian hieroglyphics, a picture script unutilized for over fourteen hundred years. Dating to the time of King Ptolemy V (204–180 BC), the Rosetta Stone is inscribed in three scripts: demotic, Greek, and hieroglyphs. The Greek proved to be a translation of the ancient Egyptian language on the stone.[10]

The English physician Thomas Young (1819) and the French philologist Jean-François Champollion (1822) performed linguistic work on the stone, and they were able to decipher the hieroglyphic language. The cracking of the language was an important step. As Andrews comments, it "marked the beginning of the scientific reading of hieroglyphs and the first step toward formulation of a system of ancient Egyptian grammar, the basis of modern Egyptology." [11] Thus, this early find by the Napoleonic expedition proved to be one of the greatest discoveries ever as it opened up the world of ancient Egypt.

The decipherment of hieroglyphs not only led to the discovery of ancient Egypt as a highly civilized culture worthy of investigation; it was also seen as important for the study of the Old Testament. For example, the work of Champollion soon bore fruit with the translation of a monumental triumphal relief on the Bubastite Portal of the main temple of Amon at Karnak.[12] The relief provides striking verification of the biblical account of

---

[10] Currid, *Doing Archaeology*, 18–19.
[11] C. A. R. Andrews, "Rosetta Stone," in *Oxford Companion to Archaeology*, 620.
[12] The best reproductions of this relief are found in *The Bubastite Portal*, vol. 3 of *Reliefs and Inscriptions at Karnak* (Chicago: Oriental Institute, 1954); for more readily available photographs, see K. A. Kitchen, "Shishak's Military Campaign in Israel Confirmed," *Biblical Archaeology Review* 15/3 (1989): 32–33. For an interpretive study of the relief, see John D. Currid, *Ancient Egypt and the Old Testament* (Grand Rapids, MI: Baker, 1997), 172–202.

Shishak's invasion of Judah and Israel in the tenth century BC (see 1 Kings 14:25–26 and 2 Chron. 12:2–4). Archaeological work also began in Mesopotamia in the first half of the nineteenth century. Georges Roux comments:

> But in 1843 Paul Emile Botta, Italian-born French consul in Mosul, started at Khorsabad the first archaeological excavations in Iraq, discovered the Assyrians and opened a new era. Almost at once (1845) an Englishman, Sir Henry Layard, followed his example at Nimrud and Nineveh, and soon a number of tells were excavated.[13]

Based on these excavations, scholars began to reconstruct the history of Mesopotamia, including the lands of Assyria and Babylonia. In this early period of discovery, Mesopotamia yielded many more monuments and inscriptions relevant to the history of the Old Testament than did Egypt. For instance, the annals of Sargon II were found at this time, and the king called himself "the conqueror of Samaria and of the entire country of Israel." In these same annals, Sargon II says that he deported 27,290 upper-class citizens from Israel and replaced them with peoples from other nations. He made Israel an Assyrian province, placed a governor over it, and exacted heavy tribute from the inhabitants. Thus Israel, the northern kingdom, met its end and ceased to exist. The annals of Sargon II provide helpful information about this important period.

For the scholarship of this time, there was a general sense of innocent discovery. Certainly the researchers recognized some problems with harmonization of ancient Near Eastern history and biblical history, but there does not appear to have been a dominant hermeneutic of suspicion in the academy. When, for example, the influential Society of Biblical Archaeology was founded in 1870, one of the founding members, Samuel Birch of the British Museum, made the following remarks to the first official meeting of the society:

> It is true that these results have not been obtained without difficulties. There has been some conflict between Assyrian and Jewish history, and

---

[13] Georges Roux, *Ancient Iraq* (Baltimore: Penguin, 1976 reprint), 43.

although Assyrian scholars, dealing with the special subject of Assyria, naturally lean with favour to the information monuments of Nineveh afford, it is by no means sure that the Assyrians, especially in speaking of foreign nations, may not have recorded errors. As the research advances, the difficulty of reconciling the chronology of the Assyrians and the Jews will melt away before the additional monuments that may be acquired. There is nothing to alarm the exegetical critic in the slight discrepancies that always present themselves in the world's history when the same fact is differently recorded by the actors in some national struggle.[14]

Although Birch may be accused of naivete, in reality the most that can be said about him with certainty is that he was not prescient. For indeed, right around the corner—in fact, in an article just about to be published in the journal of Birch's own society—George Smith announced that he had discovered an Assyrian account of the flood.[15] Everything was about to change.

The Period of Suspicion Begins (1873–1905)

Although we will deal with the ancient Near Eastern flood accounts in chapter 4 of this work, it is important to mention the discovery of the Assyrian flood story because it is a watershed event in the history of ancient Near Eastern studies. Smith began his report with the following statement:

A short time back I discovered among the Assyrian tablets in the British Museum, an account of the flood; which, under the advice of our President, I now bring before the Society.[16]

After translating and commenting on the Assyrian text of the flood, Smith concluded the following:

In conclusion I would remark that this account of the Deluge opens to us a new field of inquiry in the early part of Bible history. The question has often been asked, "What is the origin of the accounts of the ante-

---

[14] Samuel Birch, "The Progress of Biblical Archaeology: An Address," *Translations of the Society of Biblical Archaeology* 1 (1872): 6.
[15] George Smith, "The Chaldean Account of the Deluge," *Transactions of the Society of Biblical Archaeology* 2 (1873): 213–234.
[16] Ibid., 213.

diluvians, with their long lives so many times greater than the longest span of human life? Where was Paradise, the abode of the first parents of mankind? From whence comes the story of the flood, of the ark, of the birds?" Various conflicting answers have been given to these important questions, while evidence on these subjects before the Greek period has been entirely wanting. The cuneiform inscriptions are now shedding a new light on these questions, and supplying material which future scholars will have to work out.[17]

This publication received immediate scholarly response, and as Alexander Heidel points out, "it created a tremendous enthusiasm throughout Europe and gave a great impetus to the study of cuneiform inscriptions in general." [18]

Many scholars of the time concluded that the Hebrew account of the flood was directly dependent on the earlier Mesopotamian texts. It is true that the Mesopotamian flood stories predate the Old Testament by centuries. So from a simple chronological consideration, these scholars inferred that the biblical flood account evolved from the Mesopotamian story. Friedrich Delitzsch is a prime example of that mind-set because he "drew sharp attention to the Babylonian ingredient in Genesis, and went on to conclude that the Bible was guilty of crass plagiarism." [19] S. R. Driver, when considering ancient Near Eastern creation accounts, argued "that we have in the first chapter of Genesis the Hebrew version of an originally Babylonian legend respecting the beginning of all things." [20]

Scholars of the later nineteenth–early twentieth centuries did not believe that the Hebrew writers merely borrowed Mesopotamian myths, leaving it at that. No, indeed; there was a second step, and that was that the biblical authors had stripped the Mesopotamian accounts of pagan elements. In other words, they had gone to great lengths to sanitize and "Yahwize" the myths. Friedrich Delitzsch, for instance, said, "the priestly scholar who composed Gen. chap. i endeavoured, of course, to remove all

[17] Ibid., 233.
[18] Alexander Heidel, *The Gilgamesh Epic and Old Testament Parallels*, 2nd ed. (Chicago: University of Chicago Press, 1949), 2.
[19] E. A. Speiser, *Genesis* (Garden City, NY: Doubleday, 1964), lv–lvi.
[20] S. R. Driver, *The Book of Genesis* (London: Methuen, 1907), 30.

possible mythological features of this creation story." [21] Driver concluded that "no archaeologist questions that the Biblical cosmogony, however altered and stripped of its original polytheism is, in its main outlines, derived from Babylonia." [22]

Although they believed that the biblical accounts of creation and the flood were stripped of their original polytheism and of many other pagan elements, many of these early scholars believed that some remnants of those elements remained in the text. A classic example is the contention that the word *tehom* ("deep") in Genesis 1:2 is a remnant of Mesopotamian myth. Supposedly it relates to Tiamat, the goddess of the deep sea who was a foe of the creator-god Marduk. In the Mesopotamian account, Marduk had to vanquish Tiamat in order to bring about creation. Delitzsch commented,

> The priestly author that wrote the first chapter of Genesis took infinite pains to eliminate all mythological features from his story of the creation of the world. But since his story begins with the gloomy, watery chaos which bears precisely the same name as Tiamat, namely *Tehom*, . . . it will be seen that there is a very close relationship between the Biblical and the Babylonian story of the creation of the world. [23]

This connection between the two accounts has become accepted as fact in much literature of the twentieth–twenty-first centuries, and has almost reached the status of a sacred cow in some quarters. [24]

New Horizons (1906–1940)

Discovery of other cultures of the ancient Near East and their literatures came more slowly than in the cases of Egypt and Mesopotamia. Canaanite culture, for example, was known primarily from the Bible prior to the discovery of the Ugaritic texts at Ras Shamra beginning with the excavations

---

[21] Friedrich Delitzsch, *Babel and Bible* (New York: Putnam, 1903), 50.

[22] Driver, *Book of Genesis*, 30.

[23] Delitzsch, *Babel and Bible*, 45.

[24] See, e.g., Richard A. Muller, *The Study of Theology* (Grand Rapids, MI: Zondervan, 1991), 76. Muller concludes from this supposed parallel that "we learn how the fundamental monotheism of Israel interpreted and, in effect, demythologized the world-order." In chapter 3 of this present work I will respond to this apparent parallel.

there in 1929 and following. The parallels between the Old Testament and the literature of Ras Shamra are ubiquitous. I will not consider them at this point because the final chapter of this book is a study of the relationship between Ugarit and Israel.

An important year in ancient Near Eastern studies was 1906, when excavations began at the Hittite city of Bogazkoy (Hattusa). There archaeologists discovered thousands of inscriptions in several languages that make it possible for historians to piece together the basic history and culture of the Hittites. Hugo Winkler, the chief archaeologist, uncovered the royal Hittite archives, in which approximately 10,000 clay tablets were found. Some of these were written in the Akkadian language, but most were in Hittite. Within ten years of its discovery, the Hittite language had been deciphered. The Oriental Institute of the University of Chicago started the Chicago Hittite Dictionary (CHD) project in 1975, and it has made great strides in formulating a complete dictionary of the Hittite language.

One factor that played a considerable role in nineteenth-century ancient Near Eastern studies was the desire of the investigators "of making discoveries that would throw light on biblical history." [25] That was no longer the case in the twentieth century, as researchers began studying cultures of the ancient Near East on their own merits and for their own sakes.[26] The German excavations at Bogazkoy are an example of this latter trend. This shift does not mean, however, that the remains found at Bogazkoy did not shed light on the Old Testament, only that it was not a primary purpose of the investigation. For example, George Mendenhall did some groundbreaking work by demonstrating the striking parallels between the covenant forms in the Old Testament and the covenant-treaties found in the Hittite archives at Bogazkoy from the fifteenth–thirteenth centuries BC.[27]

During this period, ancient Near Eastern studies were given a

---

[25] K. A. Kitchen, *Ancient Orient and Old Testament* (Chicago: InterVarsity Press, 1966), 21.

[26] For an overview of the trends in the history of archaeology, see William F. Albright, *The Archaeology of Palestine* (Harmondsworth, UK: Penguin, 1949); and Currid, *Doing Archaeology*.

[27] George E. Mendenhall, "Covenant Forms in Israelite Tradition," *Biblical Archaeologist* 17 (1954): 50–76. A vast amount of literature has been added since Mendenhall first did his work: see, e.g., Meredith G. Kline, *Treaty of the Great King: The Covenant Structure of Deuteronomy* (Grand Rapids, MI: Eerdmans, 1963); Kitchen, *Ancient Orient*, 90–102; and Thomas McComiskey, *Covenants of Promise* (Downers Grove, IL: InterVarsity Press, 1987).

continuous supply of new literature as archaeologists uncovered major cuneiform archives. One of these came from the site of Nuzi, which was excavated between 1925 and 1933.[28] Nuzi was a Hurrian administrative center located in modern northern Iraq, and the excavations revealed thousands of tablets dealing with the administration of the city. These documents covered a wide range of topics, including politics, religion, and law.[29] Although not a goal of the excavations, the literature found at Nuzi does enlighten our understanding of biblical history. The Nuzi documents describe customs of the Hurrians that were similar to the practices of the early Hebrews such as Abraham, Isaac, and Jacob. In particular, they give a picture of inheritance rights, marriage practices, and adoption customs that parallel those in use during the patriarchal period of Israel's history.

Thousands of tablets were also uncovered from the Middle Bronze II levels at Mari, a large site in western Mesopotamia. The excavations, begun in the 1930s, found some 20,000 cuneiform tablets in the archives of the city's main palace.[30] A majority of the documents are economic and administrative in nature. The setting described by the Mari tablets is quite similar to the patriarchal period of biblical history.[31] For instance,

> . . . both portray a dimorphic society, that is, a social dichotomy between tribal chieftains, like Abraham, and powerful urban centers. This is evidenced in both Genesis and the Mari texts by customs of economic exchanges between the city dwellers and nomads, the concept of "resident aliens," and the common practice of camping in the vicinity of towns. The social structures in both literatures are organized the same way with three tiers: extended family, clan, and tribe. Other customs are quite similar, such as census taking, inheritance laws, covenant oaths, and the prominence of genealogies. The same personal and place names are found in the literary corpus of each culture: for example, Haran and Nahor.[32]

---

[28] Richard F. S. Starr, *Nuzi: Report on the Excavations at Yorgan Tepa near Kirkuk, Iraq*, vol. 1 (Cambridge, MA: Harvard University Press, 1939).
[29] M. P. Maidman, "Nuzi: Portrait of an Ancient Mesopotamian Town," in *Civilizations of the Ancient Near East*, ed. Jack Sasson, vol. 1 (New York: Scribner's, 1995), 931–947.
[30] Ch.-F. Jean, *Six campagnes de Fouilles a Mari 1933–1939*, vol. 9 of Cahiers de la Nouvelle Revue theologique (Paris: Casterman, 1952).
[31] See, e.g., Abraham Malamat, *Mari and the Early Israelite Experience*, 1984 Schweich Lectures (Oxford: Oxford University Press, 1989); idem, *Mari and the Bible* (Leiden, Netherlands: Brill, 1998).
[32] John D. Currid and David P. Barrett, *Crossway ESV Bible Atlas* (Wheaton, IL: Crossway, 2010), 63–64.

Consequently, the period encompassing most of the first half of the twentieth century was one of discovery. Thousands upon thousands of tablets were found in various languages mostly unknown before this time. In addition, the first areas of discovery in the ancient Near East from the nineteenth century—in Egypt and Mesopotamia—continued to supply more and more linguistic information to aid scholars in understanding and reconstructing their cultures. Archaeology was helpful in these tasks as it came of age as a discipline in the time between the two world wars. It "jettisoned, for the most part, any image it had of mere treasure-hunting." [33] The field developed sophisticated techniques and methodology in excavation, as well as scholarly competence. [34]

The Age of Synthesis (1945–Present)

Since the end of the Second World War, discovery of new languages and cultures in the ancient Near East has slowed down considerably. The great exception is the finding of an archive at Ebla (Tell Mardikh) in 1976. [35] The site, located in northern Syria, was the center of a thriving civilization during the second half of the third millennium BC. It was destroyed in the twenty-third century BC. The Eblaite archive was enormous, and the study of the tablets indicated that the people of Ebla had their own language, and it is the oldest West Semitic language known.

When the Ebla tablets were first discovered, there were raised expectations that numerous parallels would be found between them and the biblical text, in particular with the Genesis account of the patriarchal period. However, this avenue of research has been a disappointment. The tablets provide only a general cultural background to the late third millennium BC, and parallels with the Bible have been limited primarily to geography, place-names, and people's names. In reality, this should not be surprising since the writing of the Ebla tablets precedes the time of Abraham by at least 450 years. Translation of the texts is far from complete, and one can only hope that further work will produce further parallels.

---

[33] Currid, *Doing Archaeology*, 30.
[34] William G. Dever, "Archaeological Method in Israel: A Continuing Revolution," *Biblical Archaeologist* 43 (1980): 40–48.
[35] Paolo Matthiae, *Ebla: An Empire Rediscovered* (New York: Doubleday, 1981).

The modern period of study, since the middle of the last century, has been one of building on the discoveries made in earlier times. Incredible advances have been made in linguistic study of various languages of the ancient Near East. For example, major dictionaries have appeared or are in the process of publication for all the known languages of the ancient Near East.[36] This explosion of information, of course, has led to academic specialization. I think, for instance, of the study of the Ugaritic language: there is so much being published that it is difficult for any scholar to keep up with the information being produced.[37] Thus, the reality is that no scholar in ancient Near Eastern studies today can master all the material of the various cultures and languages of the area.

Partly due to the scholarly specialization, the question of the relationship of the Old Testament and ancient Near Eastern civilizations has become less relevant. And when it is dealt with by modern scholarship, it is often met with deep cynicism:

> The history of Israel, in many scholars' estimation, is really nothing more than a Judaic *Iliad*, *Odyssey*, or even *Winnie-the-Pooh*. One is not hard-pressed to find this perspective in recent literature about the Old Testament. Consider, for example, the conclusion of Thomas L. Thompson: "We have seen that the biblical chronologies are not grounded on historical memory, but are rather based on a very late theological schema that presupposes a very unhistorical world-view. Those efforts to use the biblical narratives for a reconstruction of the history of the Near East, in a manner comparable to the use of the archives at Mari and similar finds, can justly be dismissed as fundamentalist."[38]

While Thompson may be considered radical in his views, the reality is that modern scholarship commonly views biblical history as invention and propaganda. In other words, it was written by post-exilic authors who

---

[36] See, e.g., *The Assyrian Dictionary of the Oriental Institute of the University of Chicago* (CAD) and *The Chicago Hittite Dictionary Project* (CHD), which are massive works that are both nearing completion. For Egyptian, see, e.g., Raymond O. Faulkner, *Concise Dictionary of Middle Egyptian* (Oxford: Griffith Institute, 2009); and for Ugaritic, see Gregorio del Olmo Lete and Joaquin Sanmartin, *A Dictionary of the Ugaritic Language in the Alphabetic Tradition* (Leiden, Netherlands: Brill, 2004).
[37] A list of major journals publishing in Ugaritic studies include the following: *Aula Orientalis, Journal of the Ancient Near Eastern Society, Journal of Near Eastern Studies, Journal of Northwest Semitic Languages, Maarav, Newsletter for Ugaritic Studies, Studi epigrafici e linguistici,* and *Ugarit-Forschungen.*
[38] Currid, *Ancient Egypt and the Old Testament,* 172–173.

had limited access to true historical resources.[39] And, obviously, a majority believe that the antediluvian accounts of Genesis 1–11 are mere myth and legend, just like similar stories throughout the ancient Near East.

In evangelical Old Testament studies today there appears to be a clear drift away from the position that holds to an original, singular, and unique worldview on the part of the Hebrews.[40] For example, in regard to the book of Genesis, Peter Enns argues that we ought to "acknowledge that the Genesis story is firmly rooted in the worldview of its time."[41] And he adds, "Are the early stories in the Old Testament to be judged on the basis of the standards of modern historical inquiry and scientific precision, things that ancient peoples were not at all aware of? Is it not likely that God would have allowed his word to come to the ancient Israelites according to standards *they* understood, or are modern standards of truth and error so universal that we should expect premodern cultures to have understood them? The former position is, I feel, better suited for solving this problem."[42] John Walton frames the perspective with great clarity when he says of the Hebrew Bible, "No passage offers a scientific perspective that was not common to the Old World science of antiquity."[43] The reality for Walton and others today is that the early accounts of Genesis are "culturally descriptive rather than revealed truth."[44] To the point, many evangelical Old Testament scholars emphasize the similarities and parallels between ancient Near Eastern literature and biblical writings, and they do not recognize, to any great degree, the foundational differences between the two.

---

[39] See, e.g., John Van Seters, *Abraham in History and Tradition* (New Haven, CT: Yale University Press, 1975); idem, *In Search of History: Historiography in the Ancient World and the Origins of Biblical History* (New Haven, CT: Yale University Press, 1983); and idem, *Prologue to History: The Yahwist as Historian in Genesis* (Louisville: Westminster/John Knox, 1992).

[40] I am thinking here of authors such as Peter Enns, *Inspiration and Incarnation: Evangelicals and the Problem of the Old Testament* (Grand Rapids, MI: Baker, 2005); and John H. Walton, *Genesis*, NIV Application Commentary (Grand Rapids, MI: Zondervan, 2001).

[41] Enns, *Inspiration and Incarnation*, 27.

[42] Ibid., 41.

[43] John H. Walton, *The Lost World of Genesis One: Ancient Cosmology and the Origins Debate* (Downers Grove, IL: InterVarsity Press, 2009), 19.

[44] Ibid., 18.

2

The Nature of Polemical Thought and Writing

In the study of the relationship of Hebrew religion and culture with the environment of the ancient Near East, one of the most neglected areas of research is what can be termed *polemical theology*. We will begin by defining that term, and then we will explore a few concrete examples of it as it appears in the Old Testament. *Polemical theology* is the use by biblical writers of the thought forms and stories that were common in ancient Near Eastern culture, while filling them with radically new meaning. The biblical authors take well-known expressions and motifs from the ancient Near Eastern milieu and apply them to the person and work of Yahweh, and not to the other gods of the ancient world. Polemical theology rejects any encroachment of false gods into orthodox belief; there is an absolute intolerance of polytheism. Polemical theology is monotheistic to the very core.

The primary purpose of polemical theology is to demonstrate emphatically and graphically the distinctions between the worldview of the Hebrews and the beliefs and practices of the rest of the ancient Near East.[1] It helps to show that Hebrew thought is not a mere mouthpiece of other ancient Near Eastern cultures. Even the notorious higher critic Hermann

---

[1] See the discussion in John D. Currid, "The Hebrew World-and-Life View," in *Revolutions in WorldView*, ed. W. A. Hoffecker (Phillipsburg, NJ: P & R, 2007), 37–70.

Gunkel recognized this fact when he commented, "How incomparably superior the Hebrew legend is to the Babylonian! . . . And this also we may say, that the Babylonian legend strongly impresses us by its barbaric character, whereas the Hebrew legend is far nearer and more human to us."[2] Although I sharply disagree with Gunkel's portrayal of Hebrew writing as legend, I affirm his statement of the unique Hebrew conception of the universe and its workings. Polemical theology is one way in which the biblical writers demonstrate that uniqueness. The purpose of polemical theology is to demonstrate the essential *distinctions* between Hebrew thought and ancient Near Eastern beliefs and practices.

With that definition in mind, let us examine some brief and straightforward examples of polemical theology at work in the Old Testament. The examples are divided into two categories: polemical expressions and polemical motifs. We begin with the most basic level of polemic, that is, the idiomatic parallel, and we will observe three instances of this type of polemic at work in the text.

Polemical Expressions

A STRONG HAND

Some common expressions found in ancient Egyptian texts to describe the power of Pharaoh over his foes are that the monarch had "a strong hand," or "he possessed a strong arm," or he was "the one who destroyed his enemies with his arm." It is polemical and ironic that the author of the book of Exodus assigns the same features to Yahweh as he humiliates and destroys Pharaoh and Egypt (Ex. 3:19–20; 6:1; 7:4; 15:6, etc.).[3] James Hoffmeier comments on this parallel, asking, "what better way for the Exodus traditions to describe God's victory over Pharaoh, and as a result his superiority, than to use Hebrew derivations or counterparts to Egyptian expressions that symbolized Egyptian royal power?"[4]

In one sense, the Hebrew writers are "guilty" of borrowing expres-

---

[2] Quoted in Friedrich Delitzsch, *Babel and Bible* (Chicago: Open Court, 1903), 136.
[3] For an in-depth study of this parallel, see David R. Seely, "The Image of the Hand of God in the Exodus Traditions," (PhD diss., University of Michigan, 1990).
[4] James K. Hoffmeier, "The Arm of God versus the Arm of Pharaoh in the Exodus Narratives," *Biblica* 67 (1986): 387.

sions and concepts from the surrounding cultures. The idioms mentioned above are characteristically used of Pharaoh in Egyptian writings throughout the history of that land. Yet the biblical writers employ such borrowing for the purpose of taunting. The Hebrew authors use polemic to call into question the power of Pharaoh, and to underscore the true might of Yahweh!

THUS SAYS

An additional clear example of a parallel usage of idiomatic expression appears in Exodus 5.[5] In that chapter both Yahweh and Pharaoh give mandates introduced by the idiom "Thus says . . ." (Ex. 5:1, 10). The Egyptians were well aware of the use of that expression to preface the very commands of a deity. Their own texts, such as the Book of the Dead, frequently introduced the will of the gods with the words "Thus says . . ." For example, the 175th chapter of the Book of the Dead concludes the speech of the god by saying, "Thus says Atum." [6] The ironic use of this idiom by the biblical writer in Exodus 5 sets the stage for the ensuing confrontation between the gods of Egypt (including Pharaoh) and the God of the Hebrews. This parallel is a conscious criticism of Pharaonic sovereignty: only Yahweh is God, and only his word truly and always comes to pass.

THE HEAVENLY RIDER

Another important example of an idiomatic parallel occurs in Isaiah 19. Verses 1–15 of the chapter are an oracle by the prophet against the nation of Egypt. The opening verse draws the reader's attention immediately because it focuses on Yahweh's menacing arrival in Egypt:

> Behold, the LORD is riding on a swift cloud
>   and comes to Egypt;
> and the idols of Egypt will tremble at his presence,
>   and the heart of the Egyptians will melt within them.

---

[5] See the full development of this idea in John D. Currid, *Ancient Egypt and the Old Testament* (Grand Rapids, MI: Baker, 1997), 83.

[6] See "The Primeval Establishment of Order," in *Ancient Near Eastern Texts Relating to the Old Testament*, ed. James B. Pritchard, 3rd ed. (Princeton, NJ: Princeton University Press, 1969), 9–10.

The picture of Yahweh as one who rides on the clouds is not unique to Israelite culture (cf. Ps 104:3). Ugaritic literature, which dates to the four-teenth–twelfth centuries BC, uses the same epithet to describe the Canaan-ite storm-god Baal. It declares:

> Seven years Baal will fail
> Eight years the rider of the clouds, no dew, no rain.[7]

Given the poetic parallelism of the two lines, the attribute "rider of the clouds" is to be ascribed to the pagan god Baal.

How are we to understand the same epithet being used for two differ-ent gods, and the fact that the pagan reference appears centuries before the Hebrew citation? Some scholars argue that this is evidence that Yahweh somehow evolved from Baal, or that perhaps there is some type of syn-cretism at work here. In reality, it is more likely that the biblical author of Isaiah is making an implicit criticism of Baalism: Baal does not ride on the clouds; Yahweh does! Certainly that meaning would have been clear to the Israelites of the time, who were living in the land of Canaan and were quite knowledgeable of Canaanite culture.

The point of connection of these three polemical examples is compara-tive linguistics and particularly the parallel usages of idiomatic expressions. Many polemical parallels, however, go far beyond mere linguistic affinity. Numerous events and motifs of the Old Testament record can be seen and understood as polemics against ancient Near Eastern life and culture. At this time we will look at three examples of this larger polemical category.

Polemical Motifs

THE SERPENT CONFRONTATION

Exodus 7:8–13 relates the story of Moses and Aaron changing their staff into a serpent.[8] This activity by the Hebrew leaders is an attack on Pharaoh and the Egyptians, and it strikes at the very heart of Egyptian belief. In the first place, on the front of Pharaoh's crown was an enraged female serpent/

---

[7] Translated by the author from *I Aqht* 42–44.
[8] For an extended discussion of this passage, see John D. Currid, "The Egyptian Setting of the 'Serpent Confrontation' in Exodus 7:8–13," *Biblische Zeitschrift* 39 (1995): 203–224.

cobra called a *uraeus*. The Egyptians believed this serpent was energized with divine potency and sovereignty. It was considered the very emblem of Pharaoh's power; it symbolized his deification and majesty. "When Moses had Aaron fling the rod-snake before Pharaoh, he was directly assaulting that token of Pharaonic sovereignty—the scene was one of polemical taunting. When Aaron's rod swallowed the staffs of the Egyptian magicians, Pharaonic deity and omnipotence were being denounced and rejected outright. . . . Yahweh alone was in control of the entire episode." [9]

Second, the casting down of the rod was a challenge to the power of Egyptian magic as described in many of Egypt's mythological texts. Egyptian documents are loaded with examples of priests and magicians performing extraordinary feats, including changing inanimate objects into animals. The Westcar Papyrus, for example, tells the story of a lector-priest who makes a wax crocodile come to life by throwing it into a lake. [10] Later, he bends down, picks up the crocodile, and it becomes wax again. In the narration of the historical incident of Exodus 7, the biblical author is perhaps subtly pointing to the fictional character of Egyptian mythological texts. Moses and Aaron truly performed what Egyptian myths merely imagined. Myth became fact.

Finally, the textual evidence from Egypt demonstrates that the Egyptians had great pride in their power to manipulate venomous creatures. The two Hebrew leaders thus humiliated and defeated the magicians in something that traditionally rendered glory to the Egyptians. As Hengstenberg remarks, "Moses was furnished with power to perform that which the Egyptian magicians most especially gloried in and by which they most of all supported their authority." [11]

DROUGHT

When the great Hebrew prophet Elijah makes his first appearance in Scripture, he is pictured confronting Ahab, the king of Israel. The prophet

---

[9] Currid, *Ancient Egypt and the Old Testament*, 94.
[10] Adolf Erman, *The Literature of the Ancient Egyptians* (New York: Dutton, 1927), xxix, lxviii–lxix; William K. Simpson, *The Literature of Ancient Egypt* (New Haven, CT: Yale University Press, 1973), 15–30.
[11] Ernst W. Hengstenberg, *Egypt and the Book of Moses* (Edinburgh: Thomas Clark, 1845), 98.

pronounces a curse upon Israel in the name of Yahweh, that "there shall be neither dew nor rain these years, except by my word" (1 Kings 17:1). Drought is the promised punishment for a covenant-breaking Israel (Deut. 11:16–17). Israel, under the leadership of Ahab and Jezebel, has become Baal-saturated. Baal worship predominates throughout the land. Paganism reigns in these dark times. Thus, the Lord brings judgment on the entire nation for its apostasy.

It is critical to note that the form of punishment is lack of rain. This is purposeful and a directed curse: Israel has been worshiping Baal, who is the Canaanite god of storms and rain. The reality is that Baal does not control those elements of nature; only Yahweh does. Elijah demonstrates that truth when he says that rain will not return unless it comes by his word. It will not appear by the word of the priests of Baal, nor by the word of Ahab, nor by the word of Jezebel—only by the word of the prophet of Yahweh. Yahweh alone directs the weather, by his sovereign hand.

THE THUNDERING DEITY

One of the great pictures in the Old Testament demonstrating Yahweh's presence with his people is his thundering forth from the clouds and causing the earth to tremble at his appearance. For example, Yahweh appears in this way at the critical event of the revelation at Mount Sinai.[12] We read,

> On the morning of the third day there were thunders and lightnings and a thick cloud on the mountain and a very loud trumpet blast, so that all the people in the camp trembled. . . . Mount Sinai was wrapped in smoke because the LORD had descended on it in fire. The smoke of it went up like the smoke of a kiln, and the whole mountain trembled greatly. (Ex. 19:16, 18)

Ugaritic literature employs similar imagery for the theophany or appearance of the Canaanite storm-god Baal. For instance, one text says,

> Then Baal opened a slit in the clouds,
> Baal sounded his holy voice,

---

[12] 1 Kings 19:11–12 is another powerful example of God appearing in this way.

Baal thundered from his lips . . .
The earth's high places shook.[13]

A common scholarly interpretation of this parallel is that it proves syncretism. Michael Coogan, for example, says that "the character of the god of Israel is thus a composite; while Yahweh is primarily an El figure, many of the images and formulae that distinguish him from El are adopted from the theology of Baal." [14] Such a parallel, however, hardly proves dependence or borrowing. It could just as easily be coincidental or, as is more likely, a purposeful polemic of the biblical author against pagan Canaanite belief. In other words, it is not Baal but Yahweh who thunders from the top of the mountain and causes the earth to quake. Indeed,

The mountains quaked before the LORD,
even Sinai before the LORD, the God of Israel. (Judg. 5:5)

Some scholars downplay the role of polemical theology as an important factor in the proper interpretation of the Old Testament.[15] To the contrary, I would argue that many of the parallels between ancient Near Eastern literature and the Old Testament, from creation accounts to flood stories, may be properly and fully understood only through the right use of polemical theology. In this regard, I would wholeheartedly agree with Bruce Waltke when he says that the biblical authors "refuted the pagan myths by identifying the holy Lord as the true Creator and Ruler of the cosmos and of history." [16] The biblical writers often use polemical theology to counter ancient pagan myths that are noxious to the Hebrew faith centered on monotheism. The purpose of this book is to demonstrate to the reader the value of a right understanding of polemical theology to a good and proper interpretation of the Old Testament.

One important caveat for us to realize is that polemical theology is only one lens through which to view the relationship between the Old

---

[13] Quoted in Michael D. Coogan, *Stories from Ancient Canaan* (Philadelphia: Westminster, 1978), 21.
[14] Ibid., 20.
[15] See, for example, C. John Collins, *Did Adam and Eve Really Exist? Who They Were and Why You Should Care* (Wheaton, IL: Crossway, 2011), 137–160, in which he argues that Genesis is a "very gentle" polemic against alternate ancient Near Eastern worldview stories.
[16] Bruce K. Waltke, *An Old Testament Theology* (Grand Rapids, MI: Zondervan, 2007), 200.

Testament and ancient Near Eastern literature. So, for example, there is no question that the Hebrews and the Egyptians borrowed many things from each other that did not have a polemical angle. "One needs only consider the interrelationship of the Hebrew and Egyptian languages and vocabularies." [17] In addition, numerous cultural and religious practices were similar as well. Thus, for instance, the taxation systems of Solomon and of the Egyptian monarch Shoshenk I were quite similar because there certainly was an institutional connection between the two. What is not clear is who influenced the other, although I lean to the position of Alberto Green, who argues that Shoshenk I modeled his levy system after that of Solomon.[18] In any event, there are many ways to examine and study the relationship between the Bible and other ancient Near Eastern texts. Polemical theology, in my estimation, is one of the more important ones. It helps to highlight the distinctiveness and uniqueness of the Hebrew worldview over against the dominant setting of the rest of the ancient Near East.

---

[17] Currid, *Ancient Egypt and the Old Testament*, 26. For a good overview of many of these linguistic contacts, see Thomas O. Lambdin, "Egyptian Loan Words in the Old Testament," *Journal of the American Oriental Society* 73 (1953): 145–155; R. J. Williams, "Egypt and Israel," in *The Legacy of Egypt*, ed. John R. Harris, 2nd ed. (Oxford: Clarendon, 1971), 257–290; and idem, "Some Egyptianisms in the Old Testament," in *Studies in Honor of John A. Wilson*, Studies in Ancient Oriental Civilization 35 (Chicago: University of Chicago Press, 1969), 93–98.

[18] Alberto R. Green, "Israelite Influence at Shishak's Court," *Bulletin of the American Schools of Oriental Research* 233 (1979): 59–62.

3

Genesis 1 and Other Ancient Near Eastern Creation Accounts

It has been evident for a long time now that there are a magnitude of parallels between Genesis 1 and creation accounts from Mesopotamia and Egypt. I will attempt to demonstrate many of these similarities in the present chapter. The question at the forefront of academia for the last century and a half in regard to this issue is, how does one account for these many similarities? For many scholars, the numerous parallels prove that the Genesis record is directly dependent on earlier Mesopotamian and Egyptian texts. This position has dominated scholarly circles since the late nineteenth century. For example, Friedrich Delitzsch, in his famous book *Babel und Bibel*, went so far as to conclude that the Bible "was guilty of crass plagiarism." [1] S. R. Driver got to the point when he said "that we have in the first chapter of Genesis the Hebrew version of an originally Babylonian legend respecting the beginning of all things." [2] Hermann Gunkel argued that many biblical texts "show the path along which the Marduk myth was transformed into Genesis 1." [3] The scholarly consensus that the Hebrew creation story derived from and was considerably dependent on

---

[1] Friedrich Delitzsch, *Babel und Bibel: Ein Vortrag* (Leipzig: Hinrichs, 1902; for an English translation, see idem, *Babel and Bible* (New York: Putnam, 1903).

[2] S. R. Driver, *The Book of Genesis* (London: Methuen, 1907), 30.

[3] Hermann Gunkel, "The Influence of Babylonian Mythology upon the Biblical Creation Story," in *Creation in the Old Testament*, ed. Bernhard W. Anderson (London: SPCK, 1984), 46–47.

other ancient Near Eastern creation accounts has become almost a *shibboleth* in biblical studies.

Modern evangelicals do not agree with Delitzsch and other source critics in regard to the relationship of Genesis 1 to other ancient Near Eastern cosmogonies. Recently, however, this opposition has begun to drift and wane. Peter Enns, for instance, does hold to the uniqueness of Scripture to a degree but, in reality, not to the degree that one would hope for. He claims that we ought to "acknowledge that the Genesis story is firmly rooted in the worldview of its time." [4] And he adds, ". . . the opening chapters of Genesis participate in a worldview that the earliest Israelites shared with their Mesopotamian neighbors. . . . the stories of Genesis had a context within which they were first understood. And that context was not a modern scientific one but an ancient mythic one." [5] In this regard, John Walton agrees when he says, "Our first proposition is that Genesis 1 is ancient cosmology. . . . In these ways, and many others, they thought about the cosmos in much the same way that anyone in the ancient world thought, and not at all like anyone thinks today." [6]

Bruce Waltke describes the process of how the writer of Genesis would have used ancient Near Eastern stories of creation in the following way: "Inspired by the Holy Spirit, the biblical authors stripped the ancient pagan literatures of their mythological elements, infused them with the sublimities of their God, and refuted the pagan myths by identifying the holy Lord as the true Creator and Ruler of the cosmos and of history." [7] The Genesis writer, therefore, employed a form of *demythologization* to rid the ancient Near Eastern cosmogonies of their mythic elements, and then he would have infused into the text a monotheistic orthodoxy. In other words, the Genesis author was simply sanitizing an originally mythic text, and later reconfigured it into a historical narrative of true,

---

[4] Peter Enns, *Inspiration and Incarnation: Evangelicals and the Problem of the Old Testament* (Grand Rapids, MI: Baker, 2005), 27. Collins, *Did Adam and Eve Really Exist?*, 26 n. 4, provides an important caution when reading Enns and others. He says that these authors use words such as "worldview" in a different way than is commonly understood. One, therefore, needs to be careful with assuming common definitions.

[5] Ibid., 55.

[6] John H. Walton, *The Lost World of Genesis One: Ancient Cosmology and the Origins Debate* (Downers Grove, IL: InterVarsity Press, 2009), 16.

[7] Bruce K. Waltke, *An Old Testament Theology* (Grand Rapids, MI: Zondervan, 2007), 200.

monotheistic religion. Frankly, there is nothing new here. As previously noted, at the beginning of the twentieth century, Friedrich Delitzsch commented that "the priestly scholar who composed Gen. chap. i endeavoured, of course, to remove all possible mythological features of this creation story."[8]

Many scholars from various positions in biblical studies argue that the original mythic character of Genesis can still be seen in the "cleansed" text. For example, it is often argued that the plurality of the name of God (*'elohim*) in Genesis 1 suggests an original polytheism that only later evolved into an ardent monotheism. Similar claims are made about another key word from the creation account:

> Delitzsch and others also contend that the word *tehom* ("deep") in Genesis 1:2 is a remnant of Mesopotamian myth. Supposedly it relates to Tiamat, the goddess of the deep sea who was a foe of the creator-god Marduk. In the Babylonian creation account Marduk defeats her, divides her, and forms her into the earth, sea, and heavens. Lying behind the account of God's creation in Genesis 1, therefore, is the Mesopotamian myth that he conquered the chaos deity Tiamat and then created the universe. All the evidence, say many scholars, suggests that the biblical writer was merely demythologizing the pagan world-order. This suggestion has become fact in much recent literature.[9]

We must strongly question, however, whether the position that the Bible demythologizes ancient Near Eastern legends is the only and proper way to understand the relationship between the two literatures. It seems to me that this position emphasizes the symbiotic relationship between Genesis 1 and other ancient Near Eastern cosmogonies to the detriment of the uniqueness and distinctiveness of the biblical record. It undervalues and undercuts the originality and exceptional nature of the Hebrew world-and-life view. Thus sits the question in a nutshell: is the Hebrew creation account distinct thought at its very core or not? Is it merely another ancient Near Eastern myth that has been cleansed, or is it a radical, unique cosmogonical view? Or is it something in between?

---

[8] Delitzsch, *Babel and Bible*, 50.
[9] John D. Currid, *Ancient Egypt and the Old Testament* (Grand Rapids, MI: Baker, 1997), 28–29.

Parallels between Genesis and Ancient Near Eastern Creation Accounts

Ever since the discovery of Mesopotamian cosmogonic texts in the nineteenth century, scholars have laid great stress on their parallels with the early chapters of Genesis.[10] Indeed, important parallels do exist between the two; however, one wonders whether these parallels have not been overly emphasized to the detriment of cosmogonic parallels among other societies of the ancient Near East. As Wilfred Lambert comments, "Parallels to Genesis can indeed be sought and found there [i.e., Mesopotamia], but they can also be sought and found among the Canaanites, the ancient Egyptians, the Hurrians, the Hittites and the early Greeks. When the parallels have been found, the question of dependence, if any, has to be approached with an open mind." [11] Some recent studies, in particular, have tried to demonstrate that the cosmogonic writings of Egypt may have some striking parallels with Genesis.[12] A useful starting point, however, regarding the similarity in content between the Bible and ancient Near Eastern cosmogonies, is with the well-known Mesopotamian text called the Enuma Elish.

The Enuma Elish teaches that the creation began as a cosmic struggle between order and chaos. The opening lines of the account are as follows:

> When a sky above had not (yet even) been mentioned,
> (And) the name of firm ground below had not [yet even] been
>   thought of;
> (When) only primeval Apsu, their begetter,
> And Mummu and Tiamat—she who gave birth to them all—
> Were mingling their waters in one;
> When no bog had formed (and) no island could be found;
> When no god whosoever had appeared,
> Had been named by name, had been determined as to (his) lot,
> Then gods were formed within them.[13]

---

[10] For an overview of the discovery of these texts, see W. G. Lambert and A. R. Millard, *Atra-hasis: The Babylonian Story of the Flood* (Oxford: Clarendon, 1969), 1–5.

[11] W. G. Lambert, "A New Look at the Babylonian Background of Genesis," *Journal of Theological Studies* 16 (1965): 287–300.

[12] James K. Hoffmeier, "Some Thoughts on Genesis 1 and 2 and Egyptian Cosmology," *Journal of the Ancient Near Eastern Society* 15 (1983): 39–49; and John D. Currid, "An Examination of the Egyptian Background of the Genesis Cosmogony," *Biblische Zeitschrift* 204/4 (1991): 18–40.

[13] Thorkild Jacobsen, "Mesopotamia: The Cosmos as a State," in Henri Frankfort et al., *Before Philosophy* (Baltimore: Penguin, 1973 reprint), 184.

The watery chaos consisted of three gods, and two of these deities, Apsu and Tiamat, created a host of other gods through sexual procreation. Each of the created gods represented an important and vital element of nature (e.g., sky, water, earth). These gods desired order, whereas Apsu and Tiamat wanted mere inactivity that resulted in chaos.

A cosmic battle ensued between the gods of order and the gods of chaos. Marduk, the king of the gods of order, slew Tiamat in a fierce battle. After defeating her, Marduk used Tiamat's remains to create the cosmos. Marduk's work included the creation of a firmament, dry land, and luminaries. Finally, he created humanity:

> Blood I will mass and cause bones to be,
> I will establish a savage, "man" shall be his name.
> Verily, savage-man I will create.
> He shall be charged with the service of the gods,
> That they might be at ease!

Alexander Heidel has done a masterful job analyzing the parallels between the Enuma Elish and Genesis 1:1–2:3, and he argues that the order of creation is essentially the same where there occur points of contact.[14] He charts the order in the following way:[15]

Enuma Elish	Genesis
Divine spirit and cosmic matter are coexistent and coeternal	Divine spirit creates cosmic matter and exists independently of it
Primeval chaos; Tiamat enveloped in darkness	The earth a desolate waste, with darkness covering the deep (*tehom*)
Light emanating from the gods	Light created
The creation of the firmament	The creation of the firmament
The creation of dry land	The creation of dry land

---

[14] Alexander Heidel, *The Babylonian Genesis*, 2nd ed. (Chicago: University of Chicago Press, 1951), 129.

[15] Curiously, when Waltke provides this table in his *An Old Testament Theology*, 198, he changes the topmost righthand box to read "Divine spirit and cosmic matter coexist." One wonders why he would do that unless there is a subtle denial of the creation of matter in Genesis 1.

Enuma Elish	Genesis
The creation of the luminaries	The creation of the luminaries
The creation of man	The creation of man
The gods rest and celebrate	God rests and sanctifies the seventh day

Parallels between Egyptian creation accounts and Genesis are less known, but they have recently come under greater scrutiny.[16] The similarities between the two are worth noting. The ancient Egyptians believed that life originated from preexistent primordial waters (Nun), and this concept of a watery chaos is akin to the opening of the Enuma Elish. Primeval hillocks or mounds first appeared in these waters, and upon one of them the creator-god Re came into being through an act of self-generation. Re consequently brought order out of chaos by taking control of the eight preexistent gods, such as Kuk, who represented darkness. In this myth, the sun-god subsequently called into being other gods, who like himself represented different elements of nature.

There are a variety of accounts of how Re created the other gods who are personified in the various parts of creation. "One account pictures him squatting on a primeval hillock, pondering and inventing names for various parts of his own body. As he named each part, a new god sprang into existence. Another legend portrays Re as violently expelling other gods from his own body, possibly by sneezing or spitting. A third myth describes him creating the gods Shu and Tefnut by an act of masturbation. These gods in turn gave birth to other gods."[17] Re, however, is not the only god portrayed as creator in ancient Egypt. For example, the Memphite Theology depicts Ptah as a potter creating the universe.[18] In another text, the "Great Hymn to Khnum," the god Khnum is pictured as forming everything—man, gods,

---

[16] See J. P. Allen, *Genesis in Egypt: The Philosophy of Ancient Egyptian Creation Accounts* (New Haven, CT: Yale Egyptological Seminar, 1988).

[17] Currid, *Ancient Egypt and the Old Testament*, 36–37.

[18] William K. Simpson, ed., *The Literature of Ancient Egypt* (New Haven, CT: Yale University Press, 1973), 262. The Memphite theology is a cosmological system that portrays Ptah as the creator-god. The system was developed in the city of Memphis, and the theology is found in its full presentation in the Shabaka Text from c. 700 BC.

land animals, fish, birds—on his potter's wheel.[19] While the ancient Egyptians described one god as creator, various gods fulfilled that purpose in different accounts. In this regard, the warning given by John A. Wilson in 1946 still holds true today: "It is significant that a plural should be necessary, that we cannot settle down to a single codified account of beginnings. The Egyptians accepted various myths and discarded none of them." [20]

Some of the basic and fundamental parallels between Genesis 1–2 and Egyptian cosmogonies are presented in the following chart:

Egypt	Bible
One creator-god, although various gods may fill this role	One creator God
Image of creator gods crafting cosmos on potter's wheel or as a metal worker	Image of creator God crafting cosmos on potter's wheel (Isa. 29:16; 45:9; 64:8) or as a metal worker
Various means used by creator-god to create cosmos, including mere verbal fiat	God creates universe by mere verbal fiat
Creator-god creates all that exists	God creates all that exists
Creator-god overcomes chaos by creating light	God overcomes darkness and emptiness (Gen. 1:2) by creating light (v. 3)
Creator-god separates sky and earth	God separates sky and earth
Creation of vegetation	Creation of vegetation
Creation of luminaries	Creation of luminaries
Creation of fish and birds	Creation of fish and birds
Creation of land animals and mankind (in the image of the creator-god)	Creation of land animals and mankind (in the image of God)

These are merely some of the major points of similarity between the Hebrew and Egyptian accounts of creation. Others could be mentioned.[21]

---

[19] Miriam Lichtheim, *The Late Period*, vol. 3 of *Ancient Egyptian Literature* (Berkeley: University of California Press, 1980), 113.

[20] Quoted in Frankfort, *Before Philosophy*, 59.

[21] See Cyrus H. Gordon, "Khnum and El," *Scripta Hierosolymitana* 28 (1982): 203–214; and A. H. Sayce, "The Egyptian Background of Genesis 1," in *Studies Presented to F. Ll. Griffith* (London: Egypt Exploration Society, 1932), 419–423.

As I conclude elsewhere, "In any event, the fact of the matter is that the magnitude of parallels cannot be by mere chance. We dare not call this situation a freak of antiquity." [22]

So, then, what are we to surmise regarding the relationship between Genesis 1–2 and mythic ancient Near Eastern cosmogonic tales? Are we to conclude, because of the many parallels, that Genesis 1–2 is just as mythical in its intentions and meanings as these other stories? To answer these questions, we must do some further analysis. So far we have simply focused on the similarities between the accounts; we must, however, not overlook the differences. What we see is that the dissimilarities are not superfluous but are of great magnitude and import.

First, in regard to the very nature of the creator, all societies of the ancient Near East, save the Hebrews, were polytheists. The gods themselves were immanent, that is, personified in various powers and elements of the universe. These gods were not omnipotent but were restricted in power to the capacity of the natural elements they personified. In addition, the temperament of the gods often reflected human nature—so that the deities frequently acted in a depraved, perverted manner. To the contrary, the God of the Hebrews is presented as transcendent, that is, set apart from the cosmos. He works within the universe, but he is not part of it. The universe is God's creation, but it is not God. The God of Israel, moreover, does not act humanly by reflecting the flaws of human nature. Mankind is created in his image and not the other way around. He is pure, just, righteous, and true. Yahweh is holy and wholly other.

The gods of the ancient Near East were themselves created by the creator-god. This *theogony* (Greek "birth of the gods") is central to the cosmogonical myths, which were primarily concerned with the genealogies of the gods, their origins, and their positions in the pantheon and hierarchy of the gods. In contrast, Yahweh is portrayed as the sole deity of reality, eternal, and the creator of the cosmos. He did not engage in any theogonic activity. The Genesis account is radically monotheistic.

In the ancient Near Eastern myths, the most powerful gods were the

---

ones that harbored the greatest amount of magical prowess. In the Enuma Elish, for example, Marduk attained to the highest position in the cosmic order because he was a great magician. The gods put Marduk to a test to see if he was worthy to be their king. The gods laid a piece of cloth before Marduk, and then they challenged him as follows:

> "Lord, truly thy decree is first among gods.
> Say but to wreck or create; it shall be.
> Open thy mouth: the cloth will vanish!
> Speak again, and the cloth shall be whole!"

Marduk then acted on the dare:

> At the word of his mouth the cloth vanished.
> He spoke again, and the cloth was restored.
> When the gods, his fathers, saw the fruit of his word,
> Joyfully they did homage: "Marduk is king!" [23]

Magic was the ultimate power in the universe, even above the gods themselves.

The creation account of Genesis, in contrast, presents God as all-powerful, incomparable, and sovereign. "He owes nothing to the agency of another. In addition, creation did not occur as the result of a contest or a struggle between gods, as it did in the Mesopotamian myths. In the Enuma Elish myth, creation was a mere consequence of a war aimed at determining who would be the main god." [24] In Genesis 1–2, this is a question not even asked or worthy of consideration because there exists only one God, and he is all powerful.

In regard to the creation itself, there are major differences, that is, core distinctions between Genesis 1–2 and other ancient Near Eastern accounts. In the Enuma Elish and some of the Egyptian creation myths, creation begins from the primordial waters. These waters are preexistent; in other words, they are the eternal matter of all reality. The Pyramid Texts, for

---

[23] James B. Pritchard, ed., *Ancient Near Eastern Texts Relating to the Old Testament*, 2nd ed. (Princeton, NJ: Princeton University Press, 1955), 66.

[24] John D. Currid, "The Hebrew World-and-Life View," in *Revolutions in Worldview*, ed. W. A. Hoffecker (Phillipsburg, NJ: P & R, 2007), 50.

example, picture the beginning of creation taking form as a primordial island or hillock rises up out of the watery void. On that mound the creator-god Atum first created himself and then created the other gods by various means. To the contrary, Genesis 1 denies that there was any physical element in existence prior to God's creative labors. He simply created the universe *ex nihilo* ("out of nothing").[25]

Many scholars argue that the "deep" in Genesis 1:2 is a reference to primordial waters that existed prior to God's creative work. The Hebrew word for "deep" is *tehom*, and some scholars contend it is related to the Mesopotamian deity Tiamat, the goddess of the deep sea. Marduk, in Enuma Elish, vanquished Tiamat in order to create the earth, seas, and heaven. In consequence, these historians argue that Genesis 1:2 is a vestige of Mesopotamian creation mythology, and that God had to conquer this preexistent, chaotic deep before he began his creative work. In reality, the identification of *tehom* with Tiamat is dubious at best.[26] In addition, there is not even a hint of God having to do battle with the deep, and the deep is certainly not portrayed as a deity in the biblical text. The Hebrew creation account simply understands the deep as the primal world ocean that God created at the beginning of time.

The culmination of God's creative activity in Genesis 1 was the creation of mankind (1:26–28). God formed mankind as *imago Dei* ("image of God") and thus conferred upon humanity the status of ruler of the earth under the sovereignty of God. God gave mankind a privileged status over the created order. This purpose for humanity's creation is distinct from other ancient Near Eastern creation accounts. In Mesopotamian myth, the gods created mankind simply to do the labor assigned by the deities. "The Egyptians had no separate or elaborate account of the creation of humans. References to their origins are found in mere snippets or fragments of literary pieces devoted to other subjects."[27] The creation of humanity in

---

[25] See my argument for *ex nihilo* creation in *An EP Study Commentary: Genesis*, vol. 1 (Darlington, UK: Evangelical Press, 2003), 58–59. Contra Bruce K. Waltke, *Creation and Chaos* (Portland, OR: Western Conservative Baptist Seminary, 1974), 25–28; and idem, "The Creation Account in Genesis 1–3," *Bibliotheca Sacra* 132 (1975): 225–228.

[26] Heidel, *Babylonian Genesis*, 99–101.

[27] Currid, *Ancient Egypt and the Old Testament*, 37.

Egyptian cosmogony simply was not as important as it was in the Hebrew account.

The method of the creative work of the gods varies greatly throughout ancient Near Eastern texts. In Egypt, for example, there are three basic accounts of how the creator-god Re made the other gods—who are personified in the various elements of the universe. As noted, one myth pictured him as creating the gods Shu (god of the air) and Tefnut (goddess of the atmosphere) through an act of onanism (masturbation).[28] Another text had Re spitting (expectoration) as a method by which the lesser gods were created.[29] Another mythic portrayal of creation showed Re in contemplation as he invents names for the various parts of his body. As he named each part, a new god sprang into existence. In the Mesopotamian Enuma Elish, Apsu and Tiamat created the other gods through sexual procreation, as they "were mingling their waters as one." To the contrary, Genesis 1 depicts God as creating all things through the spoken word (vv. 3, 6, 8–11, 14, 20, 22, 24, 26). The Hebrew conception of creation was that one God fashioned the entire universe *ex nihilo* by means of verbal fiat, and this truth underscores the fact that God is omnipotent, sovereign, and incomparable.[30]

The style of writing of the cosmogonical texts from the ancient Near East is best described as "mythic narrative." What I mean by that term is simply that these creation accounts are legendary stories without determinable basis in fact or history. They are symbolic tales of primordial times that deal principally with the realm of the gods. They are narrative only in the sense that the stories have a linear forward movement, but they are simply ahistorical. Their purpose is to explain the order and meaning of the universe as it stands. Genesis 1–2, in contrast, bears all the markings of Hebrew historical narrative. The passage, however, describes a unique event and thus it is highly structured. It has an elevated style, yet it is still

---

[28] Pyramid Text, Utterance 527; cf., Coffin Text, Spell 245. The Pyramid Texts are a collection of religious texts from the period of the Egyptian Old Kingdom that were carved on the walls of the pyramids at Saqqara in the late third millennium BC. See J. P. Allen, ed., *The Ancient Egyptian Pyramid Texts* (Atlanta: Society of Biblical Literature, 2005). The Coffin Texts are a collection of ancient Egyptian funerary spells written on coffins, and they primarily date to the Middle Kingdom of the first half of the second millennium BC. See R. O. Faulkner, *The Ancient Egyptian Coffin Texts*, 3 vols. (Warminster, England: Aris & Philips, 2007 reprint).
[29] Pyramid Text, Utterance 600; Coffin Text, Spell 76:3–4.
[30] The Memphite Theology has some similarities to the biblical creation by verbal fiat; see Currid, *Ancient Egypt and the Old Testament*, 60–64.

historical narrative. C. John Collins perhaps has the best designation of the genre of Genesis 1–2 when he calls it "exalted prose narrative." [31] This description properly reflects the sequence, chronology, and historicity of the account, while at the same time underscoring its exceptional quality.

There are, of course, many more distinctions that could be cited between Genesis 1–2 and the other ancient Near Eastern creation accounts, but the key point is this: the differences are monumental and are so striking that they cannot be explained by a simple Hebrew cleansing of myth. J. V. K. Wilson agrees when he says, "the many obvious differences, due in large part to the fact that the essential religious concepts underlying the [Enuma Elish] epic are those of the Sumerians—the non-Semitic predecessors in Mesopotamia of the third millennium Akkadians and later Babylonians and Assyrians—weigh heavily in support of this opinion." [32] Although there are these major differences between the two, however, the question still remains: how are we to explain the many parallels that do exist between Genesis and other ancient Near Eastern creation accounts? How should we understand these correspondences?

The Polemical Angle

One of the ways to understand the biblical references in Genesis to ancient Near Eastern literature is as a polemic. At this point, I will provide three examples of this approach related to the issue at hand. First, on the fifth day of creation, Genesis 1 describes God's making of fish and birds. The text adds to the picture by saying that "God created the great sea creatures" (v. 21). The Hebrew term for these animals is *tanninim*, which can refer to large serpents, dragons, or even crocodiles. The reference in this verse to a specific kind of animal must have a specific purpose. In Canaanite literature, a large serpent or sea creature was the main enemy of the fertility god Baal. [33] The inclusion of large sea creatures in the Hebrew creation account can be seen as a polemic against that Canaanite myth. In the He-

---

[31] C. John Collins, *Genesis 1–4* (Phillipsburg, NJ: P & R, 2006), 44.

[32] J. V. K. Wilson, "The Epic of Creation," in *Documents from Old Testament Times*, ed. D. W. Thomas (New York: Harper & Row, 1958), 14.

[33] Michael D. Coogan, *Stories from Ancient Canaan* (Philadelphia: Westminster, 1978), 106–115; cf. Pritchard, *Ancient Near Eastern Texts*, 138–141.

brew account, Yahweh created the great sea creatures, and they were not in rebellion against him. Yahweh is sovereign, and he need not battle against such creatures to bring about creation.[34]

God's creation of the great sea creatures may also be a polemic against Egyptian beliefs. The Hebrew word for "great sea creature" in Genesis 1 is used in Exodus 7 in the story of the destruction of Pharaoh and the Egyptians at the hand of Yahweh (vv. 8–13). Aaron hurled a *tannin* (snake) before the Egyptian monarch, and Pharaoh's magicians responded by throwing down *tanninim* in the same place. Yahweh's *tannin* swallowed the *tanninim* of the Egyptian lector-priests. This demonstrates Yahweh's sovereignty over all *tanninim*; he sits enthroned over the universe, and Pharaoh does not!

A second example of polemic in Genesis 1 occurs on day four when God creates the luminaries and sets them in their stations in the sky (vv. 14–19). In other ancient Near Eastern creation literature, the making of the stars was part of *theogony*. *Theogony*, as we have seen, refers to the creation of the gods who are personified in the various elements of nature. So, in the Mesopotamian Enuma Elish, the creator-god Marduk "constructed stations for the great gods, fixing their astral likenesses as constellations." [35] The biblical author, on the other hand, is rigidly monotheistic and has no interest in theogony. Alexander Heidel agrees when he says, "The opening chapters of Genesis, as well as the Old Testament in general, refer to only one Creator and Maintainer of all things, one God who created and transcends all cosmic matter. In the entire Old Testament, there is not a trace of theogony, such as we find, for example, in *Enuma elish* and in Hesiod." [36]

No names are assigned to the luminaries in Genesis 1:16; they are simply called "the greater light," "the lesser light," and "the stars." [37] This clearly distinguishes Israelite religion from other ancient Near Eastern worldviews that believe those astral entities to be deities with god-names.

---

[34] See the important discussion of G. F. Hasel, "The Polemic Nature of the Genesis Cosmology," *Evangelical Quarterly* 46 (1974): 85–87.

[35] Pritchard, *Ancient Near Eastern Texts*, 67.

[36] Heidel, *Babylonian Genesis*, 97.

[37] Collins, in *Genesis 1–4*, 82–83, downplays the polemic angle in this instance. He believes the use of these titles without names is simply due to "the rhetorically high style of the narrative."

In Egypt, for instance, the sun-god in its various forms was the chief deity. In numerous texts this god is pictured as creating himself and then bringing into existence the lesser gods of the cosmos.[38] The Hebrew conception of the luminaries is that they are merely material objects with no life of their own, and they are never to be worshiped (see Deut. 4:19). As Hasel remarks, "They share in the creatureliness of all creation and have no autonomous divine quality." [39] Genesis 1:14–19 is a strong and conscious polemic against other ancient Near Eastern cultures. Gerhard von Rad has this mind-set when he says, "The entire passage vs. 14-19 breathes a strong anti-mythical pathos." [40] To the biblical writers, the luminaries are simply created things, mere material entities, and nothing else.

As is evident from our discussion thus far, water plays an important role in the cosmogony of the ancient Near East. In the Memphite Theology of ancient Egypt, for example, the creator-god Ptah is portrayed as creating the universe from the preexistent primordial waters (personified as the god Nun). This water is simply the stuff and material of creation. The Mesopotamian Enuma Elish also conceives of eternal water from which all of life originates. These waters are pictured as chaotic, and they must be overcome and defeated by the gods of order. Creation is, therefore, the result of a cosmic battle between the primeval gods of the water and the gods of order who are led by Marduk, the king of the gods.

Genesis 1 sits in stark contrast to that dark mythological polytheism. The biblical account has as its chief purpose to glorify the one Creator God who is the sole God of all reality. The water at creation (1:2) is certainly no deity, and it is not God's foe that needs to be vanquished. It is mere putty in the hands of the Creator. There is no war between Yahweh and the gods of chaos in order to bring about creation. Yahweh is sovereign, and all the elements of creation are at his beck and call. Again, Genesis 1–2 is ardently zealous for monotheism. Not only does this literature not allow the inclusion of other gods; it stridently argues against them with clear polemics.

---

[38] See Currid, *Ancient Egypt and the Old Testament*, 56–61.
[39] Hasel, "Polemic Nature," 89.
[40] Gerhard von Rad, *Genesis* (Philadelphia: Westminster, 1961), 53.

4

Ancient Near Eastern Flood Accounts and the Noahic Deluge of Genesis 6-9

Mythological stories of a great flood are found throughout the various cultures of the ancient Near East. The deluge-motif was so well known that in some stories it was a paradigm for school texts and for copyists (see discussion of Ugarit, below). The various versions of the motif, in addition, are not limited to a particular time period but are found through-out the history of the Levant, from the third to the first millennia BC. The earliest written sources come from the late third millennium BC in Sumer, in which the texts are inscribed on clay tablets. Perhaps the oldest refer-ence to a great flood is in the Sumerian King List.[1] This document is a list of rulers from ancient Sumer. It is a well-known text from antiquity, since at least sixteen copies of it, all written in Sumerian, have been found. The text appears to have been composed during the reign of Utu-hegal of Uruk in the twenty-second century BC.

In the structure of the text of the Sumerian King List, the flood serves as a chronological separation between the very earliest kings who ruled for

---

[1] Thorkild Jacobsen, *The Sumerian King List* (Chicago: University of Chicago Press, 1939); and James B. Pritchard, ed., *Ancient Near Eastern Texts Relating to the Old Testament*, 2nd ed. (Princeton, NJ: Princeton University Press, 1955), 265–266.

thousands of years and those monarchs who came later and ruled for hundreds of years. The antediluvian period contains eight kings who ruled the major cities of Sumer for 241,000 years. The document says the following:

> (Then) the flood swept over (the earth).
> After the flood had swept over (the earth) (and)
> when the kingship was lowered (again) from
> heaven, kingship was (first) in Kish.[2]

In the succeeding section, twenty-three kings are listed who reign a total of 24,510 years, which is a mere 10 percent of the length of the antediluvian monarchs. As an aside, this disparity is reminiscent of the biblical flood account: pre-flood people lived as long as 700 years and upward (Genesis 5), but after the flood life spans were greatly reduced (Genesis 11).

At this point it is my aim to provide an overview of the primary flood accounts that have been discovered in ancient Near Eastern contexts. This description will then be followed by a comparative study of these stories and the biblical flood account of Genesis 6–9. Finally, we will consider the relationship of the various accounts.

The Sumerian Flood Story

The oldest extant written flood account is the Sumerian flood story that was inscribed on a clay tablet in the early second millennium BC.[3] It belongs to the Old Babylonian period of the seventeenth century BC; however, many scholars would argue that the story itself likely goes back to the late third millennium as this text would be a mere copy of a well-known and long-standing story. The tablet was excavated in the city of Nippur in the early 1890s and was part of a large cache that included some 35,000 cuneiform tablets. The text is fragmentary: approximately two-thirds of the tablet is missing. What remains is the bottom triad of the front and the top triad of the reverse of the tablet.

---

[2] Quoted in Pritchard, *Ancient Near Eastern Texts*, 265.
[3] For translation of this text see Samuel N. Kramer, in Pritchard, *Ancient Near Eastern Texts*, 42–44. The text was first published and translated by Arno Poebel, "Historical Texts," *The University Museum, Publications of the Babylonian Section* 4/1 (1914): 9–70.

The text begins with a description of how the gods created or "fashioned the black-headed (people)"; although the latter term often refers to the Sumerians themselves, it may in this context denote all of humanity. The deities also brought into existence the animal kingdom, and vegetation went forth or "luxuriated" throughout the earth. Apparently the deities then ordained human kingship and founded cities which were ceded to or put under the tutelage of particular gods. One particular human king name Ziusudra, the hero of the flood, is told by a god that a flood will sweep over the land and "destroy the seed of mankind." This decision has been made by the assembly or pantheon of the gods, and its purpose is to put an end to human kingship. After a substantive break in the text, it is recorded that the flood sweeps over the land and it lasts for seven days and seven nights. Ziusudra, along with animals, weathers the storm inside a "giant boat" that has been sealed tightly. After the flood abates, the king opens a window of the boat, and the light of the sun enters to show that the storm has ended. The hero of the flood then leaves the boat, sacrifices an ox and a sheep, and pays homage to the gods. Finally, the gods grant Ziusudra eternal life, like "that of a god," and he settles in Dilmun, the place of the rising sun.

The Death of Bilgames

Also from the Old Babylonian period appears another Sumerian text that mentions the flood, and it is called "The Death of Bilgames" or "The Great Wild Bull Is Lying Down." It was first published by Samuel Noah Kramer in 1944 as a translation of some fragmentary texts found at Nippur.[4] Recent excavations at Tell Haddad (ancient Meturan) have brought to light further remains of the Bilgames death narratives.[5] My understanding of the narrative is that it opens with Bilgames on his death bed, and he has a dream that tells him he will die. The dream is then repeated; I agree with Niek Veldhuis who argues that this redundancy is actually the

---

[4] Samuel N. Kramer, "The Death of Gilgamesh," *Bulletin of the American Schools of Oriental Research* 94 (1944): 2–12.
[5] Antoine Cavigneaux and Farouk Al-Rawi, "New Sumerian Literary Texts from Tell Haddad (Ancient Meturan)," *Iraq* 55 (1993): 91–105.

dream coming true.[6] Urlugal, Bilgames's son, builds a tomb for his father. Bilgames at the close of the text enters the underworld in peace.

In the dream sequences, the narrative describes Bilgames striking down the great enemy Huwawa in the Cedar Forest and his travels to find Ziusudra, the hero of the flood, "in his abode." There he learns about the Great Deluge, and he is told about

> [. . .] the flood that [destroyed] the inhabited
> regions as well as all the foreign lands [. . .]

Bilgames learns that it was the gods who had brought the flood:

> so that we could destroy the seed of mankind (we said): "in our midst, you are the only man living, Ziusudra is the name of humanity living." From that day I (=Enki) swore by the life of heaven and earth, from that day I swore that mankind will not have eternal life. (lines 72–77)[7]

The Epic of Atrahasis

Another text from the Old Babylonian period (c. twentieth–seventeenth centuries BC) tells the story about the hero Atrahasis and contains a deluge story.[8] The text is known from several versions; one of the most complete comes from the reign of King Ammisaduqa of Babylonia (c. 1646–1626 BC). It consists of three tablets. The first tablet describes the creation and early history of mankind. The gods created humanity so that people might ease their burden because

> The gods' load was too great,
> The work too hard, the trouble too much . . .
> The gods dug out the Tigris river
> And then dug out the Euphrates . . .
> For 3,600 years they bore the excess,

---

[6] Niek Veldhuis, "The Solution of the Dream: A New Interpretation of Bilgames' Death," *Journal of Cuneiform Studies* 53 (2001): 133–148.

[7] Translation by Veldhuis, "Solution of the Dream," 141–142.

[8] See W. G. Lambert and A. R. Millard, *Atrahasis: The Babylonian Story of the Flood* (Winona Lake, IN: Eisenbrauns, 1999); Q. Laessoe, "The Atrahasis Epic, A Babylonian History of Mankind," *Bibliotheca Orientalis* 13 (1956): 90–102; and Jeffrey H. Tigay, *The Evolution of the Gilgamesh Epic* (Philadelphia: University of Pennsylvania Press, 1982).

Hard work, night and day,
They groaned and blamed each other.[9]

In the creation of mankind, the gods made an error by making humans immortal. As time passes, humans multiply to such a degree that they disturb
the sleep of the god Enlil, who is the head of the pantheon,

And the country was as noisy as a bellowing bull.
The god grew restless at their racket . . .
He addressed the great gods,
"The noise of mankind has become too much,
I am losing sleep over their racket.
Give the order that suruppu—disease shall break out."

The first tablet ends with the introduction of Atrahasis, who is a godly
figure. His "ear was open to his god Enki. He would speak with his god
and his god would speak with him."

In Tablet II, Enlil decides to destroy mankind by plague. However, the
plague-god is assuaged when presented offerings, and so he relents and the
plague ends. Enlil then attempts to limit humanity's growth by inflicting
them with famine, but this fails as well. Finally, the god orders a flood to
destroy all people.

Tablet III contains a description of the deluge. Atrahasis, the hero of
the account, is warned by the god Enki of the impending catastrophe. He
is commanded to build a boat, and to put his family and animals on board:

The birds flying in the heavens,
the cattle and the . . . of the cattle god,
the creatures of the steppe,
. . . he brought on board.[10]

A storm rages for seven days and nights. After the flood subsides, Atrahasis
emerges from the boat and makes an offering to the gods. The gods have
been tortured with hunger because there have been no sacrifices, and so

[9] Translation by Stephanie Dalley, *Myths from Mesopotamia* (Oxford: Oxford University Press, 1997).
[10] Translation by Benjamin R. Foster, *Before the Muses: An Anthology of Akkadian Literature*, 3rd ed.
(Bethesda: CDL Press, 2005): 227–280.

they "gathered like flies over the offering." Enlil is compelled by Enki to allow the human remnant to survive, and he tells Atrahasis that only he and his wife shall receive eternal life. From this point on, the lifespan of humanity shall be limited; however, never again shall such a "flood be brought about, but let the people last forever."

The Epic of Gilgamesh

Much of the material from the flood account of Atrahasis is later incorporated into a Babylonian narrative called the Epic of Gilgamesh. The bulk of our knowledge of the latter myth comes from twelve tablets discovered at Nineveh from the reign of Ashurbanipal (mid-seventh century BC).[11] Tablet XI of this myth contains an expanded version of the great deluge, in which the hero of the flood, Utnapishtim, relates the tale of the event to Gilgamesh. He tells how the god Ea had warned him of the approaching disaster, and that he should abandon all his possessions and build a ship in order to save his life. The boat is to be shaped like a cube, measuring 120 cubits high and wide. Utnapishtim made the boat with six decks, and each of the decks was divided into nine compartments. He then loaded the boat:

> After I had caused all my family and relations to go up into the ship,
> I caused the game of the field, the beasts of the field,
> (and) all the craftsmen to go (into it).[12]

A storm then lets loose for six days and nights. On the seventh day, the flood abates, and the ship goes aground on the top of Mount Nisir. Seven days later Utnapishtim dispatches a dove to find land, but it returns to the boat not having found a place to rest. He then sends forth a swallow, but it also returns to him. Finally, he sets free a raven, and it does not come back, which indicates that land has appeared. When the hero and the rest of the people disembark from the boat, Utnapishtim offers a sacrifice to

---

[11] For a translation and interpretation of this text, see Alexander Heidel, *The Gilgamesh Epic and Old Testament Parallels*, 2nd ed. (Chicago: University of Chicago Press, 1949); see also John Gardner and John Maier, *Gilgamesh* (New York: Vintage, 1985).

[12] Heidel, *Gilgamesh Epic*, 84.

the gods. Enlil then has mercy on Utnapishtim and his wife, and they are made immortal, that is, "like unto us gods."

Atrahasis at Ugarit

At the ancient site of Ugarit, located on the Mediterranean coast, numerous archives have been discovered that "suggest that there were large scribal schools active in the city. Noteworthy caches in this regard include archives in the residential area just east of the palace and in the southern part of the city, where at least 470 texts were discovered, including about 200 school texts including abecedaries, lexical lists, grammatical lists, and god lists." [13] Many of these classical texts were found in the House of the Tablets. Just north of this building the archaeologists uncovered a fragmentary version of the Atrahasis flood account, which probably dates to the fifteenth–fourteenth centuries BC.[14] It also appears to be a school text. The text is badly broken, but a general outline of the narrative can be discerned. It begins with a description of the gods taking counsel together to create a flood. Atrahasis then provides a first-person account of the flood (the text is badly damaged at this point). The story ends with both Atrahasis and his wife receiving immortality from the hands of the gods.

Berossos

A late version of the great flood was written by Berossos, a Babylonian priest of the god Bel, in the Greek language. It was one tale included in his history of Babylonia that was published in 278 BC during the Hellenistic period. The work has been lost to time, although sections of the deluge account have been preserved by the later Greek writers Eusebius and Polyhistor (his account is the most complete), and the Byzantine monk Syncellus.[15] According to this version of the flood story, the deity Kronos appears to Xisuthrus (= Ziusudra) in a vision and warns him of an impending

---

[13] William M. Schniedewind and Joel H. Hunt, *A Primer on Ugaritic: Language, Culture, and Literature* (Cambridge: Cambridge University Press, 2007), 9.

[14] Jean Nougayrol, *Le Palis Royal d'Ugarit IV: Textes Accadiens des Archives Sud, Mission de Ras Shamra, XI*, ed. Claude Schaeffer (Paris: Imprimerie Nationale, 1956); idem, *Textes Sumero-Accadiens des Archives et Bibliotheques Privees d'Ugarit* (Paris: P. Geuthner, 1968).

[15] See Gerald P. Verbrugghe and John M. Wickersham, *Berossos and Manetho: Introduced and Translated* (Ann Arbor: University of Michigan Press, 1997).

deluge by which mankind will be destroyed. Kronos tells him to build a boat and to place on board his family, friends, and an array of animals, including birds and quadrupeds. After the flood subsides, Xisuthrus sends forth birds, who return to him after having found no place to rest. He does this a second time after a few days' interval, and the birds return with mud on their claws/feet. He then attempts it a third time, and the birds do not return to him. The boat lands on the side of a mountain, and so all the passengers—human and animal—disembark from the vessel. Xisuthrus then makes an offering to the gods and departs, with wife and daughter, to dwell with the gods.

Parallels

In 1872, George Smith announced that he had discovered an Assyrian account of the flood among tablets that were stored in the British Museum from excavation at Nippur from the time of Ashurbanipal. He said,

> On discovering these documents, which were mutilated, I searched over all the collections of fragments of inscriptions, consisting of several thousands of smaller pieces, and ultimately recovered 80 fragments of these legends; by the aid of which I was enabled to restore nearly all the description of the flood, and considerable portions of the other legends. These tablets were originally at least twelve in number, forming one story or set of legends, the account of the flood being on the eleventh tablet.[16]

This is the initial discovery of the Epic of Gilgamesh, and it created quite a stir among scholars of the day because of its obvious parallels to the biblical account of the flood in Genesis 6–9. As Smith himself concluded, "On reviewing the evidence it is apparent that the events of the Flood narrated in the Bible and the Inscription are the same, and occur in the same order." [17]

The Epic of Gilgamesh (along with the other deluge accounts surveyed above) in some respects is nearly identical to the biblical narrative. Some of those obvious parallels are present in the following chart:

---

[16] George Smith, "The Chaldean Account of the Deluge," *Transactions of the Society of Biblical Archaeology* 2 (1873): 213–234. One needs to be careful to distinguish this scholar, who lived from 1840–1876, from George Adam Smith (1856–1942), who labored in a related field of study.

[17] Ibid., 232.

Epic-Tablet XI	Genesis
Divine warning of doom—lines 20–26	Divine warning of doom—6:12–13
Command to build ship—lines 24–31	Command to build ark—6:14–16
Hero constructs ship—lines 54–76	Noah builds ark—6:22
Utnapishtim loads ark, including his relations and animals—lines 80–85	Noah loads ark, including his family and animals—7:1–5
The gods send torrential rains—lines 90–128	Yahweh sends torrential rains—6:17; 7:11–12
The flood destroys humanity—line 133	The flood destroys humanity—7:21–22
The flood subsides—lines 129–132	The flood abates—8:1–3
The ship lands on Mount Nisir—lines 140–144	The ark settles on Mount Ararat—8:4
Utnapishtim sends forth birds—lines 146–154	Noah sends forth birds—8:6–12
Sacrifice to the gods—lines 155–161	Sacrifice to Yahweh—8:20–22
Deities bless hero—line 194	Yahweh blesses Noah—9:1

Not only are many of the details parallel, but the structure and flow of the stories are the same. Such overwhelming similitude cannot be explained as a result of mere chance or simultaneous invention. We are left with a question similar to our question in the previous chapter on the creation stories: how do we account for the many similarities between the biblical narrative of the flood and the other ancient Near Eastern stories? Clearly there is a relationship, but the question is one of defining the nature of that connection.

A Flood Account in Egypt

In the study of flood stories in the ancient Near East, little attention is placed upon Egyptian literature. Indeed, most academic eyes are trained on Mesopotamia and its records of a deluge. Ancient Egyptian literature, however, is not devoid of flood accounts. In a little-known piece, Edouard Naville reports and analyzes an account of a flood story from the ancient Egyptian *Book of the Dead*.[18] The story tells the mythic tale of the god Atum, who decides to destroy "what is on the surface of the earth by covering it with water, making it to be again Nu, the great ocean, the primitive water out of which everything originated." [19] Naville translates the words of Atum as follows:

> And further I am going to deface all I have done; this earth will become water (as an ocean) through an inundation as it was at the beginning. I am he who remains.[20]

The entire earth is to return to water as it was at the beginning of time. The cause of the flood will be the inundation of the Nile River alone. The Hebrew tradition has the water coming from two places: it will arrive as rain from the sky and from inundated waters coming from "all the fountains of the great deep" (Gen. 7:11).

There are parallels between the Egyptian story and the biblical narrative of the flood. Although the Egyptian text is badly damaged in places, the following events of the deluge may be reconstructed:

Egyptian Text	Biblical Narrative
1. The "sons of Nut" commit iniquity, perpetrate murder, attempt to usurp authority of the god Atum	1. The wickedness of mankind is great; "every intention of the thoughts of his heart was only evil continually" (Gen. 6:5)
2. Atum decides to bring the rebellion to an end	2. Yahweh decides to destroy mankind from the face of the earth (Gen. 6:6–7)
3. Destruction of all on the earth by means of a flood	3. Destruction of all on the earth by means of a flood (Gen. 6:17)
4. Flood arrives by inundation of the Nile River	4. Flood arrives by rain and inundation (Gen. 7:11)

---

[18] Edouard Naville, "A Mention of a Flood in the Book of the Dead," *Proceedings of the Society of Biblical Archaeology* 26 (1904): 251–257, 287–294.
[19] Ibid., 289.
[20] Ibid., 289.

Egyptian Text	Biblical Narrative
5. Flood is universal	5. Flood is universal (Gen. 7:4)
6. The "boat of millions" that rescues the gods from the flood	6. The ark that rescues Noah and his family from the flood (Gen. 7:1)

In our analysis of this relationship, we must recognize and acknowledge that although there are many similarities between the accounts, there are also major distinctions. And the differences that exist are not merely details of the text; they are at the deeper level of worldview, theology, and belief. In other words, the dissimilarities are profound:

1. *Theology.* As noted in the previous chapter with regard to creation stories, all the flood stories of the ancient Near East, except the Hebrew narrative, are polytheistic. In addition, these many gods often act humanly, that is, with the same desires, faults, and needs as humans. In the Epic of Gilgamesh, for example, the gods argue with one another regarding the extent and purpose of the flood (Tablet XI: 162–188). They simply snipe at one another. Some of the tales describe the flood as being a consequence of humans disturbing the sleep of the gods (the Epic of Atrahasis). Man himself has been created by the deities in order to lessen their workload. None of the gods are portrayed as omnipotent, omnipresent, or omniscient. These deities, therefore, are severely limited in what they can do, and their temperament often reflects that of humanity.

   The Genesis account, to the contrary, has only one divine actor: it is the one God who determines to bring about the flood, destroys mankind, and delivers Noah. He is in total sovereign control of the entire event from beginning to end. He wrestles with no other deity throughout the entire affair, and he does not cower before the flood as do some of the pagan gods (see discussion below).

2. *Morality.* As one reads the pagan, mythical accounts of the flood, there is a striking lack of morality in them, especially in comparison to the biblical account. The gods themselves appear petty and self-absorbed; their characters were often depraved and perverted, reflecting the debased lifestyles of humankind. Thus, as we already saw, the cause of the flood was mankind's continual disruption of the sleep of the gods. In contrast, the biblical narrative places the reason for the flood squarely on the back of humanity because of its brazen

sinfulness: "The LORD saw that the wickedness of man was great in the earth, and that every intention of the thoughts of his heart was only evil continually. . . . So the LORD said, 'I will blot out man . . .'" (Gen. 6:5, 7a). Noah was then chosen by Yahweh to construct an ark for survival because he "found favor in the eyes of the LORD" (Gen 6:8). Noah was delivered because of his righteousness and God's grace. Atrahasis and the other pagan heroes of the flood saved themselves because of their bravery and human wisdom.

3. *Covenant.* Bruce Waltke concludes that the "most radical difference in the two accounts is the Bible's investing the story with a covenant concept." [21] A covenant may be properly defined as "a bond in blood sovereignly administered." [22] In other words, a covenant is a binding contract and relationship between God and man, one that God has initiated and administered. The covenant highlights God's personal relationship with and commitment to his people (Gen. 9:8–17).

4. *Genre.* Genesis 6–9 is written as historical narrative; the flood account bears all the markings of that genre. A most important grammatical marker in biblical Hebrew is a device called a *vav-consecutive-plus-imperfect.* Often simply translated as "and it was," the device is the way in which a Hebrew writer presents events in a historical sequence. It appears commonly throughout Hebrew narrative but rarely in other genres such as poetry. In Genesis 6:5–22, that device appears at least a dozen times. Also, in Hebrew narrative the writers often employ a word that serves as a sign of the coming direct object—it is the word *'et* (Hebrew אֵת). It almost never occurs in poetry, but it is a clear, distinctive marker of historical prose. The sign of the direct object appears at least fifteen times in Genesis 6:5–22.

As mentioned in the previous chapter, the style of writing used in the cosmological texts in the ancient Near East is best described as "mythic narrative." They are legendary stories that attempt to explain the operation of the universe in terms of the lives of the gods; the deities are the important players in the way the universe runs. The gods themselves are personified in the very elements of creation. For example, one particular Canaanite cosmological text, called the myth of Baal, provides a striking picture of the Canaanite world-and-life view based on the activities of the gods.

The narrative tells of Baal (the god of rain, vegetation, and fertility) and his consort Anath (the goddess of love, fertility, and war)

[21] Bruce K. Waltke, *An Old Testament Theology* (Grand Rapids, MI: Zondervan, 2007), 291.
[22] O. Palmer Robertson, *The Christ of the Covenants* (Grand Rapids, MI: Baker, 1980), 4.

building a palace, and how the god Mot (the god of death and summer drought) kills Baal and takes him to the underworld. Anath retaliates by slaying Mot, and subsequently Baal is resurrected to reclaim his palace:

> She (Anath) seized El's son Mot.
> With a sword she split him;
> With a sieve she winnowed him;
> With fire she burned him;
> In the fields she saved him . . .
> Baal returned to his royal chair,
> To his dais, the seat of his dominion.[23]

The myth of Baal is a narrative of the actions of the gods that explain the cycle of seasons on earth. Drought blighted crops in Canaan each summer because the drought-god conquered the fertility-god Baal. But the rainy season appeared each fall because Anath slew Mot, and Baal, the god of rain, was restored to power. This legend provides for the Canaanite the *reason* for the yearly cycle of the seasons: it is the life and movement of the gods.

5. *Details.* There are, of course, numerous obvious differences between the accounts in regard to the details of names, numbers, and places. For example, the duration of the flood is not uniform in the various stories. The earliest Sumerian account and the Epic of Atrahasis have seven days and nights as the length of the deluge. The Gilgamesh account appears to have a six-day flood. None of these stores report the length of the drying up of the earth. To the contrary, the Noah story is quite detailed in its chronology of the flood and its aftermath (Gen. 7:8, 10–12, 17, 24; 8:3–5, 13).

Another example of such variations is pointed out by Nahum Sarna, who says, "Perhaps the most significant of all the distinctive features of the Torah account is that only Noah, his wife, his three sons, and their wives enter the ark, whereas in the other accounts the builders of the vessel, the boatman, relatives and friends are passengers with the hero and his family. This means that only in Genesis is the concept of a single family of man possible; indeed it is a major theme." [24]

---

[23] Quoted in Michael D. Coogan, *Stories from Ancient Canaan* (Philadelphia: Westminster, 1978), 112.
[24] Nahum M. Sarna, *Genesis*, JPS Torah Commentary (Philadelphia: Jewish Publication Society, 1989), 49.

Even with these striking differences between the biblical account of the flood and those from other ancient Near Eastern sources, the question is yet to be answered, how do we explain the similarities between the accounts? There is obviously a relationship, but how do we account for it? Critical scholars, for the most part, emphasize the similarities between the Genesis flood and the flood accounts from the rest of the ancient Near East. The biblical story, in their estimation, is fundamentally no different from the pagan, mythic narratives. As Driver comments, "There can be no doubt that the true origin of the Biblical narrative is to be found in the Babylonian story of the Flood." [25] According to this view, the Israelite authors took the well-known Babylonian legend and then "accommodated [it] to the spirit of Hebrew monotheism." [26] As noted earlier with regard to creation stories, such an understanding of the relationship has almost become a sacred cow in biblical studies.

Upon further reflection, however, not all scholars accepted the early conventional wisdom. Gerhard von Rad, writing in the 1960s, took a different approach: "A material relationship between both versions exists, of course, but one no longer assumes a direct dependence of the Biblical tradition on the Babylonian. Both versions are independent arrangements of a still older tradition . . ." [27] Peter Enns reflects this position well when he says,

> As with *Enuma Elish*, one should not conclude that the biblical account is directly dependent on these flood stories. Still, the obvious similarities between them indicates a connection on some level. Perhaps one borrowed from the other; or perhaps all of these stories have older precursors. The second option is quite possible, since, as mentioned above, there exists a Sumerian flood story that is considered older than either the Akkadian or biblical versions. In either case, the question remains how the Akkadian evidence influences our understanding of the historical nature of the biblical story. [28]

---

[25] S. R. Driver, *The Book of Genesis*, 6th ed. (London: Methuen, 1907), 103.

[26] Ibid., 107.

[27] Gerhard von Rad, *Genesis: A Commentary* (Philadelphia: Westminster, 1961), 120.

[28] Peter Enns, *Inspiration and Incarnation: Evangelicals and the Problem of the Old Testament* (Grand Rapids, MI: Baker, 2005), 29.

There is, however, another way of looking at the parallels between the biblical flood account and ancient Near Eastern myths of the deluge. The dissimilarities are so great, not only in details but in their very worldviews, that perhaps they are not dependent upon one another or an earlier common source. Von Rad comments that Israel's version ". . . is as different from the whole story as possible." [29] The uniqueness of the biblical account is a good argument for its independence from rather than its dependence on the pagan mythic texts. They are perhaps two separate traditions that stem from a historical flood. I have written elsewhere,

> If the biblical stories are true, one would be surprised not to find some references to these truths in extra-biblical literature. And indeed in ancient Near Eastern myth we do see some kernels of historical truth. However, pagan authors vulgarized or bastardized those truths—they distorted fact by dressing it up with polytheism, magic, violence, and paganism. Fact became myth. From this angle the common references would appear to support rather than deny the historicity of the biblical story.[30]

The Hebrew writers certainly would have been aware of and familiar with the pagan flood myths—those accounts appear to have been ubiquitous in the ancient Near East. Not only did they not agree with those stories, however, but there is internal evidence in the biblical text that one angle to their writing the biblical narrative was to dispute and impugn those other stories. This is the polemical wrinkle.

The Polemical Angle

As we have repeatedly seen in this study, the Genesis writer is a radical monotheist. His presentation of the flood account not only relays the event in a historical manner; it also contains harsh and radical rebukes of the pagan myths. These taunts are often subtle, but they are also purposeful. We can look at a few examples of this polemic. First, the entire biblical narrative accentuates the role of Yahweh in the episode: he is in full control of the events. Yahweh wills to destroy mankind (Gen. 6:7, 13), he determines to

---

[29] Von Rad, *Genesis*, 120.
[30] John D. Currid, *Ancient Egypt and the Old Testament* (Grand Rapids, MI: Baker, 1997), 32.

send a deluge (6:17), he saves Noah (6:18), he shuts him in the ark (7:16), he sends the flood and blots out all living creatures (7:23), and he causes the flood to subside (8:1). Yahweh governs the world. The sovereign control exercised by Yahweh over the floodwaters is in striking contrast to the reaction of the Mesopotamian gods in the Epic of Gilgamesh:

> The gods were frightened by the deluge,
> And, shrinking back, they ascended to the heaven of Anu,
> The gods cowered like dogs
> Crouched against the outer wall . . .
> The gods, all humbled, sit and weep.[31]

These pagan deities are at the mercy of nature, whereas Yahweh presides over nature with full command.

In the Epic of Gilgamesh, Utnapishtim takes a much more active role than Noah. Utnapishtim "made" his family and other humans and animals "go aboard" the ship. He was also the one who "battened up the entrance." [32] In the earlier Epic of Atrahasis, the flood hero is once again the one to seal the doorway of the ship.[33] To the contrary, in the Genesis account the animals are brought to Noah and it is Yahweh who shuts them all into the ark (7:16). These points underscore the truth of the sovereignty of God, and that the entire episode is unfolding according to his purpose and will. Yahweh is the primary actor in the story.

In the Mesopotamian accounts, the hero of the flood offers sacrifices to the gods (in the form of libations) after he disembarks from the ship. The response of the gods is one of famished desire:

> The gods smelled the savor,
> The gods smelled the sweet savor.
> The gods gathered like flies over the sacrifices.[34]

In the biblical account, Noah's sacrifice is an act of worship that is for the atonement of his sin. Yahweh "smelled the pleasing aroma" of the sacri-

---

[31] Quoted in Pritchard, *Ancient Near Eastern Texts*, 94.
[32] Ibid., 94.
[33] Ibid., 105.
[34] Quoted in Heidel, *Gilgamesh Epic*, 87.

fice, and he swore that he would never destroy mankind again by a flood (8:21–22). That phrase is idiomatic—it simply means that the Lord accepted and delighted in Noah's sacrifice. Yahweh is *not* like the pagan gods who gather around the sacrifice like flies because of their huge hunger.

I will provide one more example of polemic at work in the biblical flood account; there are other examples, but this ought to suffice to prove the point. As mentioned previously, one of the unique aspects of the Noahic flood narrative is the Lord's establishment of a covenant with Noah. As a physical sign of the reality of the covenantal relationship, Yahweh places the rainbow in the sky ("my bow in the cloud"; Gen. 9:12–13). The bow is like a billboard for all to see that God has made an enduring covenant with all living creatures.

The Hebrew term for "bow" is commonly used of a weapon of war. "It is often employed in pagan mythology to portray gods taking up the bow to engage in battle against other gods or humans. In the Mesopotamian creation legend, after Marduk destroys Tiamat and the gods of chaos by using a bow, the gods hang the bow in the sky and it becomes a constellation." [35] It is a symbol of Marduk's violent victory over the gods of chaos. To the contrary, the bow in the biblical account symbolizes peace between God and mankind.

---

[35] John D. Currid, *Genesis*, vol. 1 (Darlington, UK: Evangelical Press, 2003), 221. See Pritchard, *Ancient Near Eastern Texts*, 69.

5

Joseph, the Tale of the Two Brothers, and the "Spurned Seductress" Motif

Genesis 37–50 is a novella or short narrative tale about the life of the Hebrew patriarch Joseph. One great oddity in this short biography is the major interruption of the story that occurs in Genesis 38. This chapter is a parenthesis in the midst of the lengthy Joseph narrative. At the close of chapter 37 the biblical writer abruptly drops the Joseph account, picks up a unique, exceptional story in chapter 38, and then just as abruptly returns to the Joseph episode at the beginning of chapter 39. Chapter 38 is simply a hiccup in the Joseph pericope.

Genesis 38 describes in detail an encounter between the tribal progenitor Judah and his daughter-in-law Tamar. At the outset of the chapter Judah is pictured as a questionable character in regard to Israelite sexual laws and mores:

> It happened at that time that Judah went down from his brothers and turned aside to a certain Adullamite, whose name was Hirah. There Judah saw the daughter of a certain Canaanite whose name was Shua. He took her and went in to her. (Gen. 38:1–2)

Judah marries the Canaanite woman (v. 12), and she bears him three sons (vv. 3–5). After her death, Judah has sexual relations with a woman he thought was a prostitute (v. 15); she turns out to be his daughter-in-law Tamar, who is attempting to force Judah to act in the matter of the levirate law of Israel. The woman is impregnated by Judah, and she bears twins. The entire episode is a seamy, sordid tale.

The tale is placed in its present position so that Judah would serve as a foil to Joseph. In Genesis 39 the author returns to the story of Joseph, who almost immediately is subjected to sexual temptation from Potiphar's wife. Whereas Judah succumbs to the allurements of the Canaanites and an apparent prostitute, Joseph refuses to give in to the enticements of a married Egyptian woman. Another important distinction between the two chapters is the *leitphrase* ("leading clause") that appears four times in Genesis 39: "Yahweh was with Joseph" (vv. 2, 3, 21, 23). This statement is important to the structure of the chapter because it serves as an *inclusio* to it (i.e., bookends bracketing the chapter, in vv. 2 and 23). In other words, the chapter begins and ends with this theological declaration. Such an assertion is never made of Judah in chapter 38. All of this serves to underscore the moral and godly character of Joseph over against Judah: God is with Joseph, and therefore he behaves in an upright and just manner.

Potiphar's wife does not take the rejection well. She is a spurned seductress who turns on Joseph and falsely accuses him of attempted rape (39:14–15).

Another Foil? The "Spurned Seductress" Motif in Ancient Near Eastern Literature

The story line of the Joseph account is not unique in the literature of the ancient Near East; it is in fact a *leitmotif*, that is, a recurring theme. In ancient Egypt, for instance, a similar tale exists, called "The Tale of the Two Brothers." It is a "folk tale [that] tells how a conscientious young man was falsely accused of a proposal of adultery by the wife of his elder brother, after he had actually rejected her advances. This part of the story has general similarity to the story of Joseph and Potiphar's wife."[1] Before

---

[1] John A. Wilson, "The Story of the Two Brothers," in *Ancient Near Eastern Texts Relating to the Old Testament*, ed. James B. Pritchard, 2nd ed. (Princeton, NJ: Princeton University Press, 1955), 23.

considering the possible relationship between the two texts, we need to take a detailed look at the parallels between them.

The Tale of the Two Brothers[2]

This Egyptian story is fully preserved on the Papyrus D'Orbiney, currently housed in the British Museum. The manuscript dates to the reign of Seti II during the Nineteenth Dynasty of the New Kingdom (1214–1204 BC).[3] A few brief notes written at the end of the document mention the name of Sethos-Merneptah, who was the crown prince during the reign of Seti II. The date of the manuscript is inferred from this marker. On the end of the papyrus is a colophon that "makes it clear that the papyrus was written as a literary exercise by the pupil-scribe Ennana." [4] Ennana or Enene was a scribe working in the city of Memphis during the thirteenth and twelfth centuries BC. "Enene, Treasury scribe and subordinate to the Treasury scribe Kageb, produced five scrolls of scholastic miscellanies that have survived, as well as a single manuscript, the D'Orbiney Papyrus, containing the Tale of the Two Brothers." [5]

The text contains a number of corrupt passages. They are likely a result of the papyrus serving as a practice text or literary exercise by the scribe. Because of its nature as a copyist piece, the story itself probably goes back to an earlier time. The style of this tale was popular during the entire New Kingdom (1550–1070 BC), and it is less formal than the style of these types of stories during the Middle Kingdom (2040–1640 BC). It is my contention, then, that the Tale of the Two Brothers perhaps originated in the early part of the New Kingdom period.

The story revolves around two main characters: the brothers Anubis and Bata. These are names of two gods in ancient Egypt, and that probably indicates that the story truly has a mythological setting.[6] It is simply a ficti-

---

[2] For an excellent study of this piece, see Susan T. Hollis, *The Ancient Egyptian "Tale of the Two Brothers"* (Norman, OK: University of Oklahoma Press, 1990).

[3] See Miriam Lichtheim, *The New Kingdom*, vol. 2 of *Ancient Egyptian Literature* (Berkeley: University of California Press, 1976), 203–211. The text is also preserved in a late form in the Papyrus Jumilhac; see Jacques Vandier, *Le Papyrus Jumilhac* (Paris: CNRS, 1961).

[4] D. Winton Thomas, *Documents from Old Testament Times* (New York: Harper & Row, 1958), 168.

[5] A. Roccati, "Scribes," in *The Egyptians*, ed. Sergio Donadoni (Chicago: University of Chicago Press, 1997), 79.

[6] Anubis is the jackal-headed god connected with the act of mummification. Bata is a cow goddess associated with Upper Egypt.

tious account or folk tale. Edward Wente comments that it "may have been written simply for entertainment as a sort of fairy tale, [as] it draws richly upon mythological and folkloristic themes." [7] It has been suggested that because the Egyptian Tale of the Two Brothers is a mere fable, it may be assumed that the parallel story of Joseph and Potiphar's wife in the Bible must also be fictitious.[8] This, however, is a non sequitur; parallels and similarities between two stories do not necessarily determine the genre or historicity of either story.[9] There is no reason one cannot be myth and the other historical narrative.

The tale begins by presenting a pleasant, idyllic scene of an Egyptian household, consisting of the characters Anubis, his wife, and his brother Bata. The Edenic picture is soon shattered as the conscientious, hard-working Bata is falsely accused of sexually attacking his older brother's wife. He had, in reality, spurned her advances. Anubis believes his lying wife, turns against Bata, and forces his brother to leave the family. He later finds out the truth, kills his wife, and "casts her to the dogs."

There is a second segment of the tale that begins with the words "Now many days later . . .". This subsequent story tells of Bata meeting the Ennead as they are out walking and surveying the land of Egypt.[10] These gods decide to create a wife for Bata. She, however, spurns Bata and rather takes up with the Pharaoh of Egypt. Bata attempts to win her back by taking on a series of different forms, the first being a cedar tree. Bata's wife has no interest, and so she orders the cedar to be cut down. Once it is chopped down, Bata "fell dead that very instant." Then, however, he resurrects in the form of a bull, yet he meets a similar fate when the Pharaoh has him sacrificed. Bata is not finished: he comes back again, this time as a pair of persea trees. Bata's wife is again not impressed, and she orders the two trees to be cut down "and made into fine furniture." A splinter from the tree flies into her mouth, "she swallowed [it] and became

---

[7] E. F. Wente, "The Tale of the Two Brothers," in *The Literature of Ancient Egypt*, ed. William K. Simpson (New Haven, CT: Yale University Press, 2003), 80.

[8] See, e.g., Dorothy Irvin, "The Joseph and Moses Narratives," in *Israelite and Judaean History*, ed. John H. Hayes and J. Maxwell Miller (Philadelphia: Westminster, 1977), 180–203.

[9] See especially the comments of James K. Hoffmeier, *Israel in Egypt: The Evidence for the Authenticity of the Exodus Tradition* (Oxford: Oxford University Press, 1996), 80–81.

[10] The Ennead is a company of nine major gods of Egypt.

pregnant in the completion of a brief moment." [11] Bata is then reborn, now as her son, and becomes king of Egypt. He elevates his brother Anubis to succeed him, overcoming the catastrophes that had beset the pair, and they are thus reunited.

In our study we are most interested in the first part of the story, in which the "spurned seductress" motif is center stage. The parallels between it and the Joseph pericope in the matter of plot-motif are striking. The following parallels are worthy of our observation:

Tale of Two Brothers	Genesis 39
Paragraph 1: Bata is portrayed as diligent and hardworking. He tends to the goods and needs of his elder brother. He is trustworthy, and good at his labors. Bata was "a perfect man: there was none like him in the entire land, for a god's virility was in him."	Verses 1–6: Joseph "became a successful man . . . in the house of his . . . master"; he found favor in his master's sight. And "Joseph was handsome in form and appearance." The text twice mentions that the Lord was with Joseph, and that the Lord "caused all that he did to succeed."
Paragraphs 2–4: Bata simply goes about performing his daily chores. He is pictured as innocent and unaware as he does his duty. He is obedient, as the text says he "made all preparations that his elder brother had told him to [make]."	Verse 11: Joseph tends to the work of his Egyptian master with due diligence and integrity.
Paragraph 6: Bata's sister-in-law, who is nameless, has been watching him work. She wishes "to know him through sexual intimacy." So she grabs him and tempts him to lie with her.	Verses 7, 12: Potiphar's wife "cast her eyes on Joseph" and demands that he lie with her. She grabs him and tempts him to lie with her.
Paragraph 7: Bata responds to the proposal with great indignation. His brother fully trusts him and raised him from his youth. How could he betray Anubis? Bata scolds his sister-in-law and then leaves to work in the field.	Verses 8–9: Joseph answers Potiphar's wife by saying that her husband fully trusts Joseph. How could he betray such trust? For Joseph, this act would also be seen as "wickedness and sin against God." Joseph flees the scene.

---

[11] Wente, "Tale of the Two Brothers," 89.

Tale of Two Brothers	Genesis 39
Paragraph 8: Anubis's wife resorts to trickery and entrapment in order to cover her own tracks. She makes herself look as if she has been beaten, lies down, and pretends to be sick. When her husband comes home, she blames Bata for attempting to lie with her and then assaulting her when she refused to give in to him. She then demands that Bata be killed.	Verses 13–18: Potiphar's wife employs deceit in an attempt to prove her own innocence and Joseph's culpability. When Joseph fled the scene, he had left his cloak behind. When Potiphar comes home, his wife blames Joseph for attempting to lie with her, and she shows Potiphar the evidence.
Paragraph 9: Anubis responds with great anger, like "an Upper Egyptian panther." He then arms himself with a spear to kill Bata.	Verses 19–20: Potiphar responds with great anger and puts Joseph in prison.

At this point the two stories diverge. In the Egyptian account, Bata flees the scene with Anubis in hot pursuit. Bata, in great fear, prays to Re-Harakhti for justice and deliverance.[12] The god answers him by placing a large body of water, infested with crocodiles, between the two brothers. Bata then makes his case for innocence before his brother, and the god serves as a witness to the trial. The younger brother closes the scene by emasculating himself to demonstrate that he had done nothing to Anubis's wife. The mutilation is a self-imposed ordeal to confirm his oath before the god and his brother. Apparently Bata dies, and Anubis goes into mourning by placing his hands on his head and dirt on his body. The episode ends with Anubis going home, killing his wife, and throwing her body to the dogs.

In the biblical account, Joseph is immediately confined to prison. Yet we read that even there "Yahweh was with Joseph" (Gen. 39:21, 23). There is no mention, however, of the fate of the seductress, the wife of Potiphar.

The Deific Triangle

The "spurned seductress" motif also makes its appearance in Hittite and Mesopotamian myths in which the triangle of characters is composed of

---

[12] Re-Harakhti ("Re who is the Horus of the Two Horizons") ruled over all creation and was the chief state god of the Egyptians during the New Kingdom.

deities. The Hittite "spurned seductress" document is often simply referred to as the Elkunirsa Myth.[13] The story is a mere fragment from a larger narrative: we have in our possession only two broken sections from the account. The date of the fragments is a matter of debate. Some scholars argue for an early date (c. 1500 BC) and others for a late date (c. 1250 BC).[14] The text does not seem to be exclusively Hittite, because it employs the names of Semitic deities rather than Hittite ones. Two of the main gods of the text are Elkunirsha and his consort-wife Ashertu. The first name refers to the Canaanite god "El, creator of the earth" and the second to the Canaanite goddess Asherah or Astarte. These two deities are primary gods depicted in the tablets found at Ugarit, a major Canaanite city-state during the second millennium BC. In those tablets, El is pictured as "the King" and "Father of the gods," whereas Asherah is El's consort and the mother of the gods.[15] It is not clear whether the text before us is an original Hittite myth using Semitic deities or an original Canaanite story that has been retold by the Hittites.[16]

The broken text begins with the goddess Ashertu, the wife of El, repeatedly and forcefully demanding that the storm-god visit her in her tent and sleep with her. He persistently refuses her advances. His denials do not stop her activity, and she becomes more aggressive and harasses the storm-god. "At length, angered by his persistent refusal, the goddess gives him one last chance, and tells him that if he does not come, she will tell Elkunirsha, her husband, that the Storm-god attempted to over-power her. The Storm-god has no intention of acceding, but is frightened by her threat, and with an intelligence and decisiveness rare in heroes of this tale, he sets off himself as fast as possible to see the high god Elkunirsha in his tent, tell him the story, and assure him of his innocence." [17] Elkunirsha devises a plan to humble Ashertu: he tells the storm-god to sleep with his wife

---

[13] English translations of the tablet are available in A. Goetze, "El, Ashertu and the Storm-god," in Pritchard, *Ancient Near Eastern Texts*, 519; H. A. Hoffner, "The Elkunirsa Myth Reconsidered," *Revue Hittite et asianique* 23/76 (1965): 5–16; idem, *Hittite Myths* (SBLWAW 2; Atlanta: Scholars Press, 1990), 69–70.

[14] Hans G. Guterbock, "The Hittite Version of the Hurrian Kumarbi Myths: Oriental Forerunners of Hesiod," *American Journal of Archaeology* 52 (1948): 123.

[15] Michael D. Coogan, *Stories from Ancient Canaan* (Philadelphia: Westminster, 1978), 11–14.

[16] See the discussion of Lowell K. Handy, *Among the Host of Heaven: The Syro-Palestinian Pantheon as Bureaucracy* (Winona Lake, IN: Eisenbrauns, 1994), 34–37.

[17] Irvin, "Joseph and Moses Narratives," 186–187.

and to humiliate her. The storm-god obeys, he abuses Ashertu, and she responds in a rage. Although the text is broken off at this point, it appears that Ashertu is able to seek revenge and retaliate against the storm-god.

Gilgamesh Epic

The Mesopotamian story called the Epic of Gilgamesh also contains a plot-motif of the spurned seductress.[18] Tablet V of the account tells the story of Gilgamesh, traveling with his companion Enkidu, and how he cuts off the head of the dreadful Humbaba. The latter is the guardian of the Cedar Forest, and an enemy and terror to mankind. Returning from the battle, Gilgamesh refreshes himself by washing his hair, putting on clean clothes, polishing his weapons, and donning his crown (Tablet VI:1–5). The goddess Ishtar sees how handsome Gilgamesh is, and so she entices him to become her husband (VI:6–21). It is an unwelcome solicitation. Gilgamesh spurns Ishtar's advances. He does this by reviewing her past seductive and destructive ways with former husbands and lovers, and how she crushed them when she grew tired of them (VI:22–79). Ishtar responds in a rage and goes to her father Anu and her mother Antum, complaining that Gilgamesh has unjustly "enumerated mine evil deeds" (VI:85). She seeks revenge by asking her father to create a "bull of heaven" to destroy Gilgamesh (VI:92–100). Anu begrudgingly accedes to Ishtar's request and sends forth the bull to battle. In the end, the innocent hero Gilgamesh triumphs by killing the bull (VI:122–154). He and his friend Enkidu celebrate the conquest with a great and joyful banquet in the palace.

Analysis

Earlier I mentioned that Dorothy Irvin attempts to define the genre of the Joseph pericope based on the parallel of these ancient Near Eastern stories. I agree with the assessment of James Hoffmeier, who says, "I maintain that it is inappropriate to compare two pieces of literature in order to identify the genre of the one from the other unless there is good evidence that the

---

[18] Alexander Heidel, *The Gilgamesh Epic and Old Testament Parallels*, 2nd ed. (Chicago: University of Chicago Press, 1949).

texts in question were indeed commensurate, although this is not to say that we cannot compare disparate pieces of Hebrew and Egyptian literature to provide general background information." [19] Irvin's argument is similar to the assertions of those who would define Genesis 1–2 as mythic litera-ture because it has some parallels with writings like the Mesopotamian Enuma Elish that deal primarily with the realm of the gods. The fact is that Genesis 1–2 has all the markings of Hebrew historical narrative and is not presented as folklore or as mythic in any manner.

The Joseph pericope is also written in the genre of historical narra-tive, and it lacks the many mythical elements of the other ancient Near Eastern "spurned seductress" accounts. The Joseph story, like the rest of Genesis, is not being relayed by the biblical writer as a fictitious, mythic folk tale. It is a factual, historical account that serves as a polemic against the ancient Near Eastern folk tales. How is the Joseph pericope contrary to and contentious with the other Levantine accounts? And what is it relaying to the reader by employing this common plot-motif in a polemical way?

First, the "spurned seductress" stories of the Egyptians, Hittites, and Mesopotamians describe the actions of the gods and how they act hu-manly. They are much like the later tales of the Greek gods, who all have the weaknesses, emotions, and foibles of human character. Many of them simply act immorally. The Joseph story, on the other hand, relates true human behavior, and it glorifies the one true God, who is holy, righteous, and moral. He is a God who acts on behalf of his people. The biblical ac-count is neither mythic nor a folk tale, but plays off of ancient Near Eastern mythology to display its truthfulness. Paul Veyne states the following in regard to Christianity's response to pagan gods, but it certainly applies as well to our current study of the Hebrew view of the false gods when he says, "The goal of this polemic was . . . to banish all rivals and make it felt that the jealous God would tolerate no competition." [20]

---

[19] Hoffmeier, *Israel in Egypt*, 80.
[20] Paul Veyne, *Did the Greeks Believe in Their Myths? An Essay on Constitutive Imagination*, trans. Paula Wissing (Chicago: University of Chicago Press, 1988), 114.

6

The Birth of the Deliverer

As will become clear in our study, numerous stories from the Old Testament reflect common motifs or plot-motifs[1] of the ancient Near East. One of those motifs that is found in various cultures of the area is a birth story in which a child is under threat and danger in infancy, but he survives and grows up to become an important leader of his people. Most of these stories are mythic narratives or legends that deal with the lives of the gods or of larger-than-life human heroes. The various versions of the motif cover a long span of time: the earliest version perhaps appears as early as the end of the third millennium BC. The motif is found throughout the ancient Near East, including accounts from Mesopotamia, Egypt, and Hatti. Important for our investigation is the fact that there are striking parallels between the birth story of Moses recorded in Exodus 2:1–10 and these other stories. The question for us, once again, is how do we evaluate and understand the relationship of these ancient Near Eastern tales and the biblical narrative? Is there dependence between them? Is the biblical author merely borrowing well-known literature from the surrounding cultures and employing it for his own purposes? Is the biblical material legend, myth, or history? These and other questions will be dealt with in the course of this chapter. However, before we attempt to answer these questions, let us first

---

[1] Term used by Dorothy Irvin, "The Joseph and Moses Story," in *Israelite and Judaean History*, ed. John H. Hayes and J. Maxwell Miller (Philadelphia: Westminster, 1977), 183; she defines it as "a plot element which moves the story forward a step."

describe and consider the various accounts of the "birth of the deliverer" motif in the ancient Near East.

The Legend of Sargon

Sargon I (c. 2340–2284 BC) was a Semite who was the founder of the Akkadian empire in Mesopotamia. "He had been cupbearer to the king of Kish, but he overthrew his master and then marched his forces to Uruk. Sargon defeated Lugalzaggisi, who at that time was overlord of Sumer, and proceeded to conquer Ur, Lagash, Umma, and finally all Sumer, even to the Persian Gulf. He founded his capital at the city of Agade, the only royal city of ancient Mesopotamia whose location is unknown."[2] Sargon expanded his land holdings with military campaigns against Syria in the west and Elam to the east. He ruled more than fifty-five years, and by all accounts his reign was a glorious one.

We do not have much contemporary inscriptional evidence from the reign of Sargon; there are two Sargon texts that describe his military expansion to the east, in particular, against Elam.[3] Sargon was certainly a historical figure of great consequence, but in reality we know little of him from documents of the time. Sargon's reign, however, "made such an impression on the Sumero-Akkadians that his personality was surrounded with a lasting halo of legend."[4] Indeed, there are several literary works of a later date that speak of Sargon's life, kingship, and military exploits. The question for the historian is, how much of the later literature is mere legend and how much of it contains true historical detail?

One of these later texts is the Legend of Sargon, and it tells of Sargon's birth and his rise to power.[5] Four copies of the text have been discovered (Texts A, B, C, D) on tablets that come from as early as the seventh century BC. The date of the original composition is uncertain. Brian Lewis

---

[2] John D. Currid and David P. Barrett, *Crossway ESV Bible Atlas* (Wheaton, IL: Crossway, 2010), 59.
[3] W. Hinz, "Persia, c. 2400–1800 B.C.," *Cambridge Ancient History*, vol. 1, chapter 23 (Cambridge: Cambridge University Press, 1963), 5–7.
[4] Georges Roux, *Ancient Iraq* (Baltimore: Penguin, 1964), 140.
[5] James B. Pritchard, ed., *Ancient Near Eastern Texts Relating to the Old Testament*, 2nd ed. (Princeton, NJ: Princeton University Press, 1955), 119. The most up-to-date and detailed study of this text is Brian Lewis, *The Sargon Legend: A Study of the Akkadian Text and the Tale of the Hero Who Was Exposed at Birth* (Cambridge, MA: American Schools of Oriental Research, 1980).

concludes, and Tremper Longman agrees, that it was originally written during the reign of Sargon II (721–705 BC) in the neo-Assyrian period.[6] The purpose of the tale was to glorify Sargon II by showing that he was a worthy successor of Sargon I of Akkad. In other words, the text was partially composed to legitimize the rule of Sargon II. That chronology certainly is possible, although it is speculative. Some of the elements of the legend are found in other texts that precede the full accounts of the seventh–sixth centuries BC. For example, one Old Babylonian text (early second millennium BC) begins, "I am Sargon, the beloved of Ishtar, who roams the entire world." [7] The idea that Sargon is the beloved one of Ishtar does not make its appearance in the Legend of Sargon, but it has been present in Mesopotamian literature for centuries. This is perhaps one indication that the composition derives from an earlier age than Sargon II. Again, to be fair, we are uncertain as to its provenance.

The text is related in the first person singular: "Sargon, the mighty king, king of Agade, am I." Obviously the story is not from the time of Sargon I, and therefore its genre is what Albert Grayson calls "pseudo-autobiography" or what Longman names as "fictional autobiography." [8] Some scholars disagree with this definition, but it is essentially correct.[9] The bottom line is that the text is fictional and legendary, as it was written long after the death of Sargon I.

The plot narrative of the story may be divided into four parts:

1. *Lines 1–3.* The tale opens with Sargon's self-identification; again, he is purported to have written this document about himself, but this is highly unlikely. Here he describes his lowly, or at least questionable, origins. He is the son of an *enetu*, that is, a high priestess.[10] Sargon never knew his father: perhaps his father had died young, or more

[6] Ibid., 97ff.; Tremper Longman, *Fictional Akkadian Autobiography: A Generic and Comparative Study* (Winona Lake, IN: Eisenbrauns, 1991), 57–58.

[7] Lewis, *Sargon Legend*, 133.

[8] Albert K. Grayson, *Babylonian Historical-Literary Texts* (Toronto: University of Toronto, 1975), 8 n. 11; and Longman, *Fictional Akkadian Autobiography*, 53–60.

[9] See Hans G. Guterbock, "Die historische Tradition und ihre literarische Gestaltung bei Babylonieren und Hethitern bis 1200," *Zeitschrift fur Assyriologie* 42 (1934): 1–91, who classifies this text as *naru*-literature. It is a literary type that is structured like accounts appearing on monumental stelae.

[10] Early translators thought this term meant a "lowly woman," but modern studies have properly rendered it as a "priestess."

likely Sargon is the product of an illegitimate relationship. Sargon's family is not well-known or well-heeled; his brothers do not live in the city or the plain but are mere highlanders. One wonders if this text is dealing with the legitimacy of Sargon's kingship, since he was a Semite and not a Sumerian. In fact, Sargon's throne name was *sarru-ken(u)*, which means "the king is legitimate."

2. *Lines 4–9.* The text now relates Sargon's birth story. Apparently at the time of his birth there exists some type of danger or peril so that his mother gives birth to him "in secret." The nature of the threat is not disclosed in the text. Whatever it is, the danger forces the mother to place Sargon in a basket of reeds, cover the basket with bitumen to seal it against destructive elements, and abandon it in "the rivers." The plural perhaps reflects the twin rivers of the Tigris and Euphrates. The tar-covered vessel is for protection from the waters, as is clear from Sargon's statement that the rivers "did not rise over me." At the close of the water ordeal, Sargon is "lifted out" of the water by a gardener named Akki, through the "goodness of his heart."

3. *Lines 10–12.* Akki then raises Sargon as his own son, and the youth becomes a gardener like his adoptive father. The text then relates that the goddess Ishtar loves Sargon in this period of his youth, and this indicates divine election and divine approval of his person.

4. *Lines 13–30.* Because of Ishtar's favor, Sargon becomes ruler and deliverer of the kingdom. Much of this section deals with Sargon's military prowess and how he expanded his kingdom over the land of Sumer and extended it as far as Lebanon to the west.

Sections 2–4 of the text, in particular lines 4–13, are clearly reminiscent of the birth account of Moses in Exodus 2:1–10. The elements of commonality are: (1) the danger and secrecy surrounding the birth; (2) the mother placing the exposed child in a reed basket covered with bitumen; (3) the abandonment of the child in a river; (4) the rescue and adoption of the child; and, finally, (5) the boy growing up to become a great leader of his people. Although some commentators disagree, it seems obvious that there is some type of relationship between the two accounts: in matters of plot, sequence, and details the stories generally match. The question before us again is, what is that relationship? How do we explain parallel stories like these appearing in different cultures and times? Is there dependence or not?

The dominant thinking in the field of biblical studies, of course, is that the story of Moses has been borrowed from the Legend of Sargon. Often the assumption is that the Legend of Sargon was composed earlier than the story of Moses, and therefore the biblical text must be dependent on the earlier ancient Near Eastern documents. That is probably a poor assumption, as James Hoffmeier rightly argues:

> A further problem for those wishing to find a correlation between the Sargon legend and the Moses birth story is, as noted above, that the earliest surviving copies of the Sargon text date from the Neo-Assyrian or later times. This factor, along with others, suggests that the legend may have been recorded by (or for) the late 8C Assyrian king, Sargon II, who took the name of his great Akkadian forebear and identified himself with that monarch. This possibility diminishes the case for the Sargon legend influencing Exodus because if we allow that J or E (usually dated to the 10C and 8C respective) is the source behind Exodus 2:1-10, and follow the traditional dating for these sources, both would predate the reign of Sargon II (721-705)." [11]

Hoffmeier's tentative conclusion that the biblical account of the birth of Moses was not dependent on the Sargon legend is predicated on the late scheme of the dating of the authorship of Exodus. If one accepts an even earlier dating of the composition of Exodus, perhaps a Mosaic authorship, then the biblical narrative predates the Sargon legend by centuries.

The Myth of Horus

As I have attempted to demonstrate, many scholars believe the birth story of Moses to be clearly related to the Legend of Sargon.[12] However, some do not agree. A few historians, to the contrary, argue that the parallels between the two accounts are weak and mere generalities. Rather, because the setting of the Moses birth narrative is Egypt, one should look for connections with the literature of *that* land. As Gary Rendsburg points out, "the nature of biblical literature suggests that we should look not to Mesopotamia to

---

[11] James K. Hoffmeier, *Israel in Egypt* (Oxford: Oxford University Press, 1999), 136–137.
[12] See B. S. Childs, "The Birth of Moses," *Journal of Biblical Literature* 84 (1965): 109–122; and B. R. Foster, "The Birth Legend of Sargon of Akkad," in *The Context of Scripture*, ed. William W. Hallo and K. Lawson Younger, Jr., vol. 1 (Leiden, Netherlands: Brill, 1997), 1:461.

explain a feature in a story set in Egypt, but rather to Egypt." [13] And a story from Egypt that contains what Donald Redford calls the "exposed-infant motif" has been found: it is commonly called the Myth of Horus.[14]

The fullest account of this birth story is found in Plutarch's *Isis and Osiris*, which was written late in his life (46–120 AD).[15] An abridged text called *P. Jumilhac* appears earlier, during the Ptolemaic period in the second century BC. Redford has complained that these texts are so late, and were probably borrowed from the Greco-Roman period, that they have no relationship to the biblical narrative. Rendsburg properly refutes Redford by arguing that "elements of the Horus-Seth conflict and the Isis-Horus relationship appear already in the Pyramid Texts from the Old Kingdom and in the Coffin Texts from the Middle Kingdom. . . . the only element of the Horus birth story that appears for the first time in late texts is the specific mention of the papyrus basket." [16] Thus, the basic story and the motif of "the exposed child" have been part of Egyptian literary culture for a long time.

The setting of the story is the realm of the gods. Two of the major figures of the account are Osiris, the deity who rules the netherworld, and his wife, Isis. The text narrates the murder of Osiris by the god Seth, the deity of disorder, deserts, storms, and war. Isis responds by resurrecting and resuscitating her husband, and then she conceives a son by him. She gives birth to Horus "in the marshlands of Chemmis." But there is great danger for Horus: his mother is afraid that if Seth discovers Horus's existence and whereabouts he will kill the child. Apparently Seth would be afraid that the child will grow up to take revenge on him for killing Horus's father, Osiris. Seth does find out about Horus's existence, and he attempts to lure Isis and her child to their death. Thoth, the god of healing and wisdom, comes to their defense, and they are able to escape back to the marshlands of Chemmis (the Delta). There Isis hides Horus in papyrus thickets, and

---

[13] Gary A. Rendsburg, "Moses as Equal to Pharaoh," in *Text, Artifact, and Image: Revealing Ancient Israelite Religion*, ed. Gary M. Beckman and Theodore J. Lewis (Providence: Brown Judaic Studies, 2006), 201–219.
[14] Donald B. Redford, "The Literary Motif of the Exposed Child," *Numen* 14 (1967): 209–228.
[15] Daniel S. Richter, "Plutarch on Isis and Osiris: Text, Cult, and Cultural Appropriation," *Transactions of the American Philological Association* 131 (2001): 191–216.
[16] Rendsburg, "Moses as Equal to Pharaoh," 206 n. 19.

in the later accounts she places him in a papyrus basket. Seth continues to try to kill Horus, even transforming himself into a snake to bite the child. Horus survives the peril, and by the end of the myth he is grown up and ready to fight Seth and to avenge the killing of his father Osiris.

The birth story of Horus, of course, is mythic; it deals with the lives of the gods. Its purpose appears to be justification for Horus's rise in becoming the first state god of Egypt. The Horus-Seth conflict in general has another purpose, and that is to demonstrate Horus's close relationship with Pharaoh as ruler of all Egypt. In the great battle between Horus and Seth, Seth either wounded or stole Horus's eye so that Horus was in a weakened condition. Eventually Horus recovered his eye, regained great strength, and conquered Seth. To the ancient Egyptian, the eye of Horus became the symbol of all the power and virtue of that deity. Accordingly, "the symbol and seal of royal power, the uraeus of the crown, is called the Eye of Horus." [17] In other words, Pharaoh's crown was imbued with all the power and virility of Horus. Pharaoh ruled the land as an incarnation of Horus (and Re).

The biblical story of the birth of Moses clearly echoes this well-known mythic narrative of the conflict between Seth and Horus and, in particular, the part of it called the Horus birth story. The basic parallels between the two are as follows:

Birth of Horus	Birth of Moses
Child in great danger: Seth attempting to kill him	Child in great danger: Pharaoh attempting to kill him (Ex. 1:15–22)
Role of mother emphasized: Isis tries to protect the child Horus	Role of mother emphasized: Jochebed tries to protect the child Moses (Ex. 2:2)
Isis hides child in papyrus thicket; later versions in a papyrus basket	Jochebed places child in a papyrus basket and hides him in a reed thicket by the banks of the Nile River (Ex. 2:3)
A second familial-related female serves as the child's guardian: Horus's aunt Nephthys	A second familial-related female serves as the child's guardian: Moses's sister, Miriam (Ex. 2:4)

---

[17] Henri Frankfort, *Kingship and the Gods* (Chicago: University of Chicago Press, 1948), 126.

Birth of Horus	Birth of Moses
Isis nurses the child	Jochebed nurses the child by arrangement with Pharaoh's daughter (Ex. 2:7–9)
The god Thoth comes to the aid of Isis and Horus	Yahweh comes to the aid of all Israel (Ex. 2:23–25)
Horus rises to become first state god of Egypt, incarnated in Pharaoh	Moses rises to become leader to deliver the people of Israel from Pharaoh's hand

The setting of the birth of Moses in Egypt is an important connection with the Myth of Horus that is not present with regard to the Legend of Sargon. The very qualities and temper of the biblical account direct us to Egypt and nowhere else. Furthermore, the biblical narrative does not appear to be anachronistic but properly reflects ancient Egyptian customs and practices. The birth account itself even includes Egyptian vocabulary. For example, after Moses is born, Jochebed could hide him no longer than three months, so she places him in a *gome' tebah* ("a basket made of bulrushes"; Ex. 2:3). The first term, *gome'*, is an Egyptian word that means "papyrus." The second word, *tebah*, is also an Egyptian loan word that literally means "chest, coffin." The ancient Egyptians were known to have used sailing vessels made of long reeds (Isa. 18:1–2), and thus this as a means to deliver the child from danger has Egypt written all over it.

Another example of a solid vocabulary connection is the naming of the child "Moses." This name derives from the Hebrew verb *mashah*, which means "to draw out," and it reflects the action of Pharaoh's daughter, who "drew him out of the water" (Ex. 2:10). However, the name is also a common Egyptian word meaning "son of." Many Egyptian names "employ it in conjunction with other words: Thutmosis (son of Thut) and Ahmosis (son of Ah), for example. In the name 'Moses', however, the genitive has no object. He is simply 'the son of.' This is probably a pun by the biblical writer to emphasize the point that Moses was not a son of Egypt, but rather a son of Israel." [18]

---

[18] John D. Currid, *Exodus*, vol. 1 (Darlington, UK: Evangelical Press, 2000), 64.

Rendsburg is correct when he concludes that "the sum of the evidence is clear: not surprisingly, a biblical story set in Egypt echoes a well-known and popular myth from Egypt." [19] The connection between the two stories is tight and clear, but we are still left with the questions from the beginning of the chapter, such as, what is the exact nature of their relationship? What is their association?

Hittite Tales

The literature of the Hittites contains at least three stories with the primary theme of the birth to the gods of a child who is in immediate and great peril. The child, however, is delivered from danger and grows up to be an important deity and leader of the gods. The first such story is called the Song of Ullikummis.[20] This story was originally Hurrian from the middle of the second millennium BC, but it is found in its fullest form on tablets from the Hittite capital of Hattusa from the fourteenth–thirteenth centuries BC. The narration tells of the deity Kumarbi, "the father of the gods," siring a son who is to grow up and seek revenge on his father's enemies among the gods. Kumarbi then hides the child with friends in the under-world so that Ishtar will "not crush him like a reed." The child, named Ullikummis, is delivered, and remains in a safe place where he will grow up in order to avenge his father. The adult Ullikummis then poses a threat to all the other gods.

A second Hittite story, called "The Sun-god and the Cow," is another birth myth.[21] It tells the story of how the Sun-god impregnated a cow, and how the cow gave birth to a two-legged calf. The cow is angry because the calf should have four legs, and so she attempts to kill it: "Like a lion, the cow opened her mouth and went toward the child to eat (it?)." [22] The Sun-

---

[19] Rendsburg, "Moses as Equal to Pharaoh," 207.

[20] Pritchard, *Ancient Near Eastern Texts*, 121–125.

[21] It is sometimes referred to as "The Tale of the Fisherman." An excellent translation appears in Harry A. Hoffner, Jr., "The Sun God and the Cow," in *The Context of Scripture*, ed. William W. Hallo and K. Lawson Younger, Jr., vol. 1 (Leiden, Netherlands: Brill, 1997), 155–156. For commentary on the text, see Hans G. Guterbock, *Kumarbi* (Zurich: Europa Verlag, 1946); idem, "The Hittite Version of the Hurrian Kumarbi Myths: Oriental Forerunners of Hesiod," *American Journal of Archaeology* 52/1 (1948): 123–134; and Harry A. Hoffner, Jr., "Hittite Mythological Texts: A Survey," in *Unity and Diversity*, ed. Hans Goedicke and J. J. M. Roberts (Baltimore: Johns Hopkins University Press, 1975), 136–145.

[22] Hoffner, "Sun God and the Cow," 155.

god, however, rescues the child and takes him to the mountains to be under the protection of some animals there. The child is eventually discovered by a childless fisherman, who takes him home. He and his wife decide to take the child and rear him, but first they plot to convince their neighbors that the child has been born to them. The story ends at this point, but it is evident that it continues on another tablet that has not been found.

The third tale is often referred to as "The City of Zalpa," and like the previous two stories it originated in the mid-second millennium BC. The bulk of the narrative is concerned with a three-generational war between Hatussa, the capital city of the Hittites, and Zalpa, a city located to the north of Hatussa in central Anatolia. At the close of the story Zalpa is destroyed. The preface to the entire account deals with primordial events that occur in the city of Kanesh. One of the events recorded is as follows:

> The queen of Kanes gave birth to thirty sons in a single year. She said, "What is this—I have produced a horde!" She caulked containers with grease, placed her sons therein, and launched them into the river. The river carried them to the sea, at the land of Zalpa. But the gods took the sons from the sea and raised them.[23]

Other Hittite myths, such as the tale "Brother Good and Brother Bad," have a similar plot-motif, but it is unnecessary that we consider each and every one of these. We need simply to recognize the ubiquitous nature of the motif in Hittite literature.

Analysis

The motif of a persecuted child is, as we have seen, a common one in the ancient Near East. In most of these stories, the basic plot of the drama is the rescue of an imperiled child who grows up to become a great leader and deliverer. The biblical narrative of Moses clearly fits into this pattern: it is a descriptive account of the persecution of a Hebrew child by the Egyptian Pharaoh, and how he is delivered and destined to become a leader and savior of the Israelites. In addition, many of the details of the Moses

---

[23] John M. Foley, ed., *A Companion to Ancient Epic* (Oxford: Blackwell, 2005), 262.

story are found in the other accounts. I have attempted to highlight many of these parallels in the study above. In my opinion, the parallels in structure, flow, and details of the accounts are not coincidental. The relationship appears obvious and certain, but what is the exact and precise nature of that association? Is there borrowing of one from another? Is there dependence?

Before considering some suggestions to help us understand that relationship, it is important that we see that there are some critical dissimilarities between the biblical account and the ancient Near Eastern stories.[24] The differences are deep and extensive, and they go to the very heart of the disparate views of the Hebrews over against the pagan peoples of the surrounding nations. The unique and exceptional character of the Hebrew world-and-life view is highlighted by such a comparison.

1. *Ancient Near Eastern fiction.* All of the birth accounts discussed above from the pagan peoples surrounding Israel are either myth or legend. In other words, they are focused on the realms of the gods or demigods or folklore heroes. Although in the case of the legends there perhaps is a kernel or two of historical fact, they are mostly devoid of what is commonly understood as history. While the birth of Moses reflects and echoes many of the elements of those stories, it is different because it does not take place in the mythic or legendary sphere. In other words, what was mere myth and legend in the ancient Near Eastern literature was true history in Israel. God truly called a deliverer and saved him from great peril, and he became savior of the people of Israel. What was myth in pagan contexts was fact in Israel. Myth became fact.

2. *Ancient Near Eastern theology.* The story of the birth and life of Moses accentuates the reality of a providential God who is separate from the universe but determines the operation of the universe. Yahweh, therefore, is both transcendent and immanent. To the contrary, the other ancient Near Eastern cosmologies sought to explain the structure and operation of the universe in terms of gods who personified nature. While ancient pagan writers speculatively searched for elements that ordered the universe internally and called them gods, the Hebrew authors presented an

---

[24] In chapter 4, I dealt with this issue in detail in regard to the flood accounts of the ancient Near East. It would serve the reader well to review that chapter. There is some obvious redundancy, but that is to be expected.

external force who created and continually sustained the cosmos. Ancient Israelite cosmology rested upon the Hebrews' unique belief in a single God (monotheism) who began the universe and was completely sovereign over its operation. The entire birth account of the deliverer Moses was played out according to Yahweh's will, purpose, and plan.

3. *Ancient Near Eastern anthropology.* The Israelite writers also understood humans to be important and essential to the workings of the universe. They were creatures of great purpose and dignity. They were made not to be slaves but to be princes, rulers, and the crown of creation. In the Hebrew birth account, humans take center stage, and they are of critical importance for the unfolding of God's redemptive history. In the pagan birth accounts, humans are superfluous (except perhaps for Sargon, who in fact becomes a demigod). In reality, a dominant anthropological theme throughout the ancient Near East is the belief that mankind was created to be slaves to the gods and to serve their every whim. Humans are mere secondary players, simple role actors, in the mythic narratives of the gods.

The Polemical Angle

Although the persecuted-child motif appears throughout the ancient Near East, it is clear that the biblical narrative of Moses's birth most closely resembles and echoes the Myth of Horus from Egypt.[25] This makes perfectly good sense, since the setting of Moses's birth is Egypt. In fact, the biblical author may have employed this echo from a well-known Egyptian myth for polemical reasons. In other words, the writer takes the famous pagan myth and turns it on its head in order to ridicule Egypt and to highlight the truth of the Hebrew world-and-life view. At the heart of the polemic is a taunt of the Egyptian Pharaoh:

> Furthermore, the biblical writer utilized the venerable Horus myth in order to present Moses as equal to Pharaoh. The young Moses is akin to the young Horus, the latter a mythic equal of the living Pharaoh. At the same time, the Pharaoh of the biblical story has been transformed from

---

[25] Hoffmeier, in *Israel in Egypt*, 139, demonstrates that the parallels are not merely thematic; there are several Egyptian loan words employed in Exodus 2:1–10. This helps to confirm the connection between the two accounts.

his Egyptian mythological position of the persecuted, that is, Horus, to that of the persecutor, that is, Seth.[26]

In other words, whereas Egyptian thought teaches that Pharaoh is the incarnation of the persecuted Horus, the biblical writer is saying that, in reality, he is not the persecuted Horus but the persecutor Seth! Moses, on the other hand, is the Horus figure who survives infant persecution to grow up and deliver his people from the evil figure of Pharaoh as the Seth figure. This ironic twist is a polemic that serves as an overwhelming assault on Pharaoh and his status as the living embodiment of the god Horus.

---

[26] Rendsburg, "Moses as Equal to Pharaoh," 207–208.

7

The Flights of Sinuhe and Moses

Much of the polemical theology we have witnessed thus far has dealt with the relationship of the stories of the Bible and ancient Near Eastern myth. Accounts of creation and of floods throughout the Fertile Crescent occur within the realms of the gods and by their very nature are fictitious and folkloristic. At the very heart of these myths are concepts such as polytheism and theogony; and, as I have attempted to demonstrate, such theological thought and underpinnings are foreign and antagonistic to the worldview of the Hebrews. The biblical authors are solidly monotheistic and Yahwistic; and there is simply no room for alien, pagan thought in Hebrew religion. Therefore, they often taunt ancient Near Eastern myth in their writings; polemics is one way of belittling and disparaging pagan myth.

Polemical theology, however, is not restricted in its use to mere mockery of myth. It can be applied to other genres as well that include historical narrative, poetry, and fictitious narrative. Here we will consider one important and prime example of polemics at work in this field: the parallel stories of Sinuhe and Exodus 2:11–22.

The Story of Sinuhe

John Van Seters correctly comments that "the story of Sinuhe is a literary work of the Middle Kingdom that may be justly described as a classic of ancient Egyptian literature." [1] The tale has been found on five papyri and on well over twenty ostraca.[2] "The numerous, if fragmentary, copies of this work testify to its great popularity, and it is justly considered the most accomplished piece of Middle Kingdom prose literature." [3] The story was popular because it underscores an Egyptian's strong love of country, loyalty to Pharaoh, and a desire to end one's days on the banks of the Nile River. In this regard, the character Sinuhe is a true son of Egypt.

The earliest manuscript of the story of Sinuhe dates to the Twelfth Dynasty of Egypt (1991–1783 BC), which is part of the Middle Kingdom period. The text relates a story that purportedly occurred during the Twelfth Dynasty at the time of the death of Pharaoh Amenemhet I (1991–1962 BC) and into the reign of his successor Senwosret I (1971–1926 BC). Thus, the composition of this earliest papyrus (called P. Berlin 3022) is close to the time of the supposed occurrence of the events it records. In addition, the narrative and its details fit the time period in question and therefore it is a credible account. Whether it is a historical account is a matter of debate. Georges Posener argues that it is a completely fictitious construction based on the model of a tomb autobiography. He says, "This composition deserves to be called a novel." [4] Others argue that it is not a tomb autobiography, but that the various elements of the text are common to other genres of Egyptian literature. No matter, the real question is to what extent does the story, real or not, reflect the historical conditions of the time of the Twelfth Dynasty in Egypt? The answer, I believe, is clear:

> On the basis of historical criticism it is possible to conclude that the story does represent rather accurately both the political conditions in Egypt at the beginning of the reign of Senwosret I—the unsettled period following the assassination of Amenemhet I—and the restoration of tranquility and political security by the end of his reign.[5]

---

[1] John Van Seters, *In Search of History* (New Haven, CT: Yale University Press, 1983), 164.
[2] An ostracon is a pottery shard with writing on it.
[3] Miriam Lichtheim, *The Old and Middle Kingdoms*, vol. 1 of *Ancient Egyptian Literature* (Berkeley: University of California Press, 1973), 222.
[4] Georges Posener, "Literature," in *The Legacy of Egypt*, ed. John R. Harris, 2nd ed. (Oxford: Clarendon, 1971), 232.
[5] Van Seters, *In Search of History*, 165–166.

At the end of the day, it seems that the best description of the literary type to which the story of Sinuhe belongs is historical fiction.[6]

The story begins with a description of Sinuhe's position as an Egyptian court official.[7] He was in the service of Nefru, the daughter of Amenemhet I and wife of his successor, Senwosret I, and therefore he was an attendant close to the throne of Egypt. At some point in his service, Sinuhe overheard some of the royal children discussing some type of plot. Although the reader is never told the object of the sedition, it is likely that it is the assassination of Amenemhet I, which took place in 1962 BC. Sinuhe's response to the plot is great fear; he says, "My heart fluttered, my arms spread out, a trembling befell all my limbs." [8] Obviously he is afraid that he will be implicated in the rebellion.

And so, Sinuhe flees Egypt. He first runs to the wilderness to the east of Egypt, and eventually ends up at a place called the "Walls of the Ruler." According to the text, this is some type of obstacle which was "made to repel the Asiatics and to crush the sand-farers." It may have referred to a huge canal that the Egyptians built, running from Pelusium on the Mediterranean Sea to Lake Timseh just to the east of the Wadi Tumilat.[9] It measures 20 meters wide at the bottom and 70 meters wide at water level. The canal was constructed either in the First Intermediate Period (c. 2134–2040 BC) or during the Middle Kingdom (c. 2040–1640 BC). Its primary function was for defense and containment—to keep Asiatics out and slaves in. In any event, Sinuhe flees to the edge of the desert, and he hides behind a bush so that he will not be seen by Egyptian guards.

Sinuhe then flees further into the wilderness, where he is on the verge of dying of thirst. A sheikh, however, gives him water and milk, and then

---

[6] Cf. John L. Foster, "Sinuhe: The Ancient Egyptian Genre of Narrative Verse," *Journal of Near Eastern Studies* 39/2 (1980): 89–117.

[7] The literature on the story of Sinuhe is vast. Aside from the well-known works on the piece, I found helpful the following: A. M. Blackmon, "The Story of Sinuhe," *Bibliotheca Aegyptica* 2 (1932): 1–41; Cyrus H. Gordon, "The Marriage and Death of Sinuhe," in *Love and Death in the Ancient Near East: Essays in Honor of Marvin H. Pope*, ed. John H. Marks and Robert M. Good (Guilford, CT: Four Quarters, 1987), 43–44; and A. F. Rainey, "The World of Sinuhe," *Israel Oriental Studies* 2 (1972): 1–40.

[8] Lichtheim, *Old and Middle Kingdoms*, 224. This is the source of all the translations that follow.

[9] A. Sneh, T. Weissbrod, and I. Perath, "Evidence for an Ancient Egyptian Frontier Canal," *American Scientist* 63 (1975): 542–548; and W. H. Shea, "A Date for the Recently Discovered Eastern Canal of Egypt," *Bulletin of the American Schools of Oriental Research* 226 (1977): 31–38.

brings him into his tribe. Sinuhe travels from there to Byblos on the Mediterranean coast, and ends up settling at Qedem. A ruler in the area gives his daughter in marriage to Sinuhe and allows him to choose a lush and good part of the land to live in. Sinuhe prospers there and spends many years raising crops and children; as he says, "I passed many years, my children became strong men, each a master of his tribe."

Yet Sinuhe has a great yearning to return to his homeland of Egypt. In his advanced years he longingly proclaims,

> May Egypt's king have mercy on me, that I may live by his mercy! May I greet the mistress of the land who is in the palace! May I hear the commands of her children! Would that my body were young again!

Word of Sinuhe's condition makes its way to the Pharaoh. When Senwosret I hears of Sinuhe's desire, he invites him to come home: "Come back to Egypt!" Sinuhe eventually returns to Egypt, and he has an audience with Pharaoh in the palace. The king greets him pleasantly, all is forgiven, and Sinuhe is accepted back into royal society. The Egyptian people build a pyramid-tomb for him and, thus, Sinuhe will finally be buried next to the Pharaoh as a true and loyal Egyptian.

Structure of the Story of Sinuhe

In an important analysis of the narrative structure of the story of Sinuhe, J. Robin King has defined ten primary steps in the sequence of the account.[10] They are:

1. Initial situation
2. Threat
3. Threat realized
4. Exile
5. Success in exile
6. Exilic *agon* [conflict]
7. Exilic victory
8. Threat overcome

---

[10] J. Robin King, "The Joseph Story and Divine Politics: A Comparative Study of a Biographic Formula from the Ancient Near East," *Journal of Biblical Literature* 106 (1987): 577–594.

9. Return and reconciliation
10. Epilogue

King compares this narrative sequence to four other ancient Near Eastern biographies: the Story of Idrimi, the Apology of Hattusilis, Esarhad-
don's Fight for the Throne, and Nabonidus and His God. He concludes
that there is a

> basic, invariable narrative pattern lying behind a certain kind of life story
> from the ancient Near East: a hero, living in an initial situation of privi-
> lege (because of his initial patron), is forced to flee from it as a result of
> a threat against him; in exile he receives support; and with the assistance
> of a divine helper he is able to return and be reconciled with his former
> community, there to live out a life in harmony with it.[11]

Of course, there exists an elasticity in the paradigm because each story
with the "exile-return" motif does not contain all ten steps of the sequence.
In addition, one step may receive more content than another, depending
on the particular story. There is room in the motif for narrative expansion
and narrative diminution.

The "Exile-return" Motif in Exodus 2

The story of Moses's flight from Egypt, recorded in Exodus 2:11–22, fits
well into the "exile-return" motif of the ancient Near East. For the most
part, the various sequential steps defined above can be easily identified in
the biblical account:

Narrative Steps	Exodus
1. Initial situation	1. Moses lives in the Egyptian royal court under the patronage of Pharaoh's daughter (Ex. 2:10)
2. Threat	2. Moses kills an Egyptian, and he is threatened with exposure by one of the Hebrew slaves (Ex. 2:11–14)

---

[11] Ibid., 584–585.

Narrative Steps	*Exodus*
3. Threat realized	3. Pharaoh seeks to kill Moses (Ex. 2:15a)
4. Exile	4. Moses flees into the wilderness (Ex. 2:15b)
5. Success in exile	5. After Moses delivers the daughters of Reuel, he marries Zipporah, has a son, and does well in the land of Midian (Ex. 2:21–22)
6. Exilic *agon* (conflict)	6. Moses has a confrontation with shepherds at a well in Midian (Ex. 2:16–17)
7. Exilic victory	7. Moses delivers Reuel's daughters from the shepherds, and he waters their flocks (Ex. 2:17)

But then, as we shall see, the points of comparison become less clear:

8. Threat overcome	8. When Moses returns to Egypt, there follows a lengthy account of the defeat of Pharaoh (Exodus 4–14)
9. Return and reconciliation	9. Moses returns to Egypt (Ex. 4:18–31)
10. Epilogue	10. Moses leads Israel out of Egypt to the land of promise (Exodus 15ff.)

Although the two stories, Sinuhe and Exodus 2:11–22, have many thematic parallels and similar details, they differ in one major area. They have strikingly contrastive endings. In this regard, a first point to consider is that when the two main figures, Sinuhe and Moses, are settled in Asia, they have opposite feelings regarding the land of Egypt. Sinuhe has a great longing and yearning to return to Egypt, the land of his birth and people. He is truly a son of Egypt. Moses, on the other hand, has no such desire. When called by God to return to Egypt, he shrinks from his calling and creates a myriad of excuses so as not to go back to Egypt (Ex. 3:11–13; 4:10–17). The reality is that Moses is not a son of Egypt. The

New Testament writer of the book of Hebrews comments on this truth when he says,

> By faith Moses, when he was grown up, refused to be called the son of Pharaoh's daughter, choosing rather to be mistreated with the people of God than to enjoy the fleeting pleasures of sin. He considered the reproach of Christ greater wealth than the treasures of Egypt, for he was looking to the reward. By faith he left Egypt . . . (11:24–27a).

Moses is truly a son of Yahweh and a son of Israel!

The biblical account of Moses's flight from and return to Egypt is, thus, acutely anti-Egyptian. The Hebrew writer, well versed in commonly known Egyptian literature, plays off of the tale of Sinuhe and turns it upside down and inside out. By use of a polemical ending, the author taunts Egypt and her nationalistic fervor: Moses doesn't crave Egypt or her kingly deity; he longs only to serve Yahweh.

8

Who Is "I Am that I Am"?
Exodus 3 and the Egyptian
Book of the Heavenly Cow

Polemical thought and writing is not monopolized by the Hebrews in ancient Near Eastern literature. It is not unique to them.[1] As in all matters of cultural contact between different people, there is cultural, literary, religious, and sociopolitical movement and exchange both ways. In this chapter we will consider a little-known parallel between Egyptian literature and the Old Testament. The Egyptian text is the Book of the Heavenly Cow. It will serve as an example of polemical theology on the part of the ancient Egyptians in response to a major theological tenet of Hebrew theology. We will begin with a basic study of that piece.

Provenance

The Egyptian text the Book of the Heavenly Cow is perhaps "the oldest extended mythical narrative from ancient Egypt."[2] It is first attested in the New Kingdom period after the Amarna period during the thirteenth

---

[1] See, for example, Michael V. Fox, "Ancient Egyptian Rhetoric," *Rhetorica* 1 (1983): 9–22; and Miriam Lichtheim, *The Old and Middle Kingdoms*, vol. 1 of *Ancient Egyptian Literature* (Berkeley: University of California Press, 1973), 3–12.

[2] William K. Simpson, ed., *The Literature of Ancient Egypt* (New Haven, CT: Yale University Press, 2003), 289.

century BC. The text is inscribed on the walls of three royal tombs of the Egyptian Nineteenth Dynasty (c. 1307–1196 BC); it is also visible today in several tombs of the Pharaohs in the Valley of Kings in Luxor. Part of the text appears in the tomb of Tutankhamen. A full copy of it has been discovered in the tomb of Seti I (c. 1300 BC).

Composition of the literary piece is, however, likely much earlier than the thirteenth century BC. The first section of the text, often referred to as "The Destruction of Mankind," is cited in the text The Teaching for Meri-kare.[3] The latter document is first attested during the First Intermediate Period (c. 2134–2040 BC). Some scholars believe that the entire document of the Book of the Heavenly Cow was probably composed in the Middle Kingdom (c. 2040–1640 BC), thus predating even the earlier date for the events of Exodus.

Genre

The style of writing of the Book of the Heavenly Cow is perhaps best defined as "mythical narrative." The subject matter of the document is mythic, that is, it deals with the realm of the gods.[4] Thus, it is neither historical nor is it taking place in time as we know it. However, it is not written in the form of poetical literature. The story has a linear forward movement, that is, historical progression, and it is composed clearly in Egyptian prose style.

The Basic Story

As noted, the opening scene of the Book of the Heavenly Cow is often referred to as "The Destruction of Mankind." This myth begins with the sun-god Re becoming aware of a plot against him that has been hatched by mankind. Re is pictured in the text as somewhat vulnerable to mankind's plotting; indeed Re,

---

[3] Ibid., 152–165. Cf. James B. Pritchard, *Ancient Near Eastern Texts Relating to the Old Testament*, 2nd ed. (Princeton, NJ: Princeton University Press, 1955), 414–418.

[4] One of the best discussions regarding the meaning of myth is found in Paul Veyne, *Did the Greeks Believe in Their Myths? An Essay on Constitutive Imagination*, trans. Paula Wissing (Chicago: University of Chicago Press, 1988). On page 14, Veyne says that "mythical tradition transmits an authentic kernel that over the ages has been overgrown with legends."

had grown old, his bones being of silver, his flesh of gold and his hair of genuine lapis lazuli. (lines 2–3)

Because of their rebellious conniving, Re has a burning desire to completely destroy mankind from the face of the earth. Re's first step in response to the sedition is to convene a meeting of the gods who had been with him when he created mankind. He tells the convention that "Mankind, who originated from my Eye, has contrived a plot against me" [5] (line 9). Re is thus seeking the counsel of the gods:

I cannot slay them until I have heard what you might have to say about this. (line 10)

The gods tell Re to send Hathor, the sky goddess, to go and deal harshly with mankind. She is to destroy them. She obeys, and she begins the slaughter in the desert lands; she is triumphant and apparently enjoys her work, as she says:

I have overpowered mankind, and it was agreeable to my heart. (line 14)

After hearing the report of the carnage, Re has second thoughts regarding the destruction of mankind. He relents from his vengeance and has compassion on the rebellious humanity. He commands Hathor to "hold off decimating them" (line 15). Re changes his mind and saves humanity from the rampaging Hathor.

The text then evolves into a creation myth. As a result of mankind's rebellion and fallen nature, Re brings the universe as we know it into being. He creates the sun, moon, and stars, and they move across the sky. In a pictographic scene accompanying the text, the Egyptians depicted this creation of the cosmos as a cow being uplifted by the god Shu, the deity of air and light, with the help of eight other deities. The modern title of the text, the Book of the Heavenly Cow, derives its name from this depiction.

---

[5] The ancient Egyptians had numerous creation myths in which various gods are pictured as creating the universe by differing methods. One Pyramid Text, Utterance 600, portrays Atum as creating the universe by expectoration or spitting. Another means described in such texts is onanism. Re apparently creates mankind from the tears of his eyes. For an overview of the Egyptian creation accounts, see John D. Currid, *Ancient Egypt and the Old Testament* (Grand Rapids, MI: Baker, 1997), 53–73.

An Extraordinary Parallel

In the last few decades, scholarship has demonstrated and underscored the truth that there are some astounding parallels between Egyptian and Hebrew religious and cultural practices. The literature on the subject is plentiful.[6] One of the most interesting parallels to date is found in the Book of the Heavenly Cow as it relates to the biblical book of Exodus.

In "The Destruction of Mankind," the opening section of the Book of the Heavenly Cow, the god Re determines that mankind will not rebel against him. He pronounces the following edict:

> I am that I am. I will not let them take action.[7]

In a brief reference to this text, Egyptologist Erik Hornung draws a connection between it and Exodus 3:14: "God said to Moses, 'I AM WHO I AM.' And he said, 'Say this to the people of Israel, "I AM has sent me to you."'"[8] The passage describes God's revelation of his name to Moses at the burning bush. Egyptologist Gerhard Fecht agrees with Hornung that a parallel is in evidence. He comments on the Egyptian text that it "recalls the Old Testament in Exodus 3:14 'I am that I am' ('ich bin, der ich bin')."[9]

Not only is there a parallel in meaning and sense of the two passages, but there is also a clear phonetic and morphological connection between them. The Hebrew divine name revealed in Exodus 3:14 is Yahweh (Hebrew *yhwh*), and it derives from the Hebrew verb "to be" (*hyh*).[10] For a

---

[6] For recent major works, see Currid, *Ancient Egypt and the Old Testament*; James K. Hoffmeier, *Israel and Egypt: The Evidence for the Authenticity of the Exodus Traditions* (Oxford: Oxford University Press, 1997); Donald B. Redford, *Egypt, Canaan, and Israel in Ancient Times* (Princeton, NJ: Princeton University Press, 1992); Nahum M. Sarna, *Exploring Exodus: The Heritage of Biblical Israel* (New York: Schocken, 1986). The reader should also consider the little-known work of Rodger W. Dalman, *A People Come Out of Egypt: Studies in the Books of Exodus, Deuteronomy, and Judges* (Conrad, MT: Send the Light Press, 2002).
[7] Or, perhaps, "I am that I am. I will not tolerate this!"
[8] See Erik Hornung, *Der Ägyptische Mythos von der Himmelskuh: Eine Ätiologie des Unvollkommenen*, vol 46 of Orbis Biblicus et Orientalis, 2nd ed. (Freiburg: Universitatsverlag; und Gottingen: Vandenhoek & Ruprecht, rev. 1991; 1997 reprint).
[9] Gerhard Fecht, "Metrische Umschreibung mit Anmerkungen zum verstandnis von Metrik und Aussage," in Hornung, *Der Ägyptische Mythos von der Himmelskuh*, 125.
[10] This name for God means "I am who I am," and it signifies, first of all, that God is self-existent. He determines his own existence and he is independent of anything else for his being. Secondly, it indicates that he is immutable, and he is not in the process of becoming something else. And finally, it implies the eternality of his being. God has always been and he always will be. "The name *yhwh* appears in the imperfect and thus, it is sometimes translated in the future: 'I will be who I will be.' The imperfect in Hebrew actually can appear in any tense, past, present, or future. It is rather to be understood as uncompleted action." See John D. Currid,

long time Egyptologists have believed that the Egyptian verb "to be" is linguistically related to the Hebrew "to be" verb. The Egyptian root word is *yw*.[11]

Both textual references are also structured according to an *idem per idem* formula. This formula literally means "the same by the same," and the use of the construction highlights the totality of Yahweh's being. In Exodus 3:14, God reveals his name to Moses as "I am who I am" (Hebrew *'hyh 'shr 'hyh*). The sun-god Re in "The Destruction of Mankind" declares himself to be the same: "I am that I am" (Egyptian *ywy ymy*).

Extrabiblical References

The appearance of the divine epithet "I am that I am" in the Book of the Heavenly Cow is the earliest instance of it in extrabiblical literature. The Hebrew divine name *yhwh* is present in other major extrabiblical texts. We will consider three of these briefly.

1. *Ketef Hinnom scrolls.*[12] In 1979, Gabriel Barkay excavated an Iron Age burial cave at Ketef Hinnom, just to the southwest of the city of Jerusalem. The tomb was a typical late Iron Age, c. late seventh century BC, burial structure. The common Judean burial at this time took place in a rock-cut cave. When a person died, the body was placed on a burial bench in the tomb along with personal items such as pottery vases, jewelry, and trinkets. Once the body decayed, the bones were placed in a repository beneath the burial bench.

When the team began to excavate the repository, they came upon two small silver scrolls. Since the scrolls were metal, the archaeologists had a difficult time unrolling and deciphering the text on each scroll. They began with the larger of the two scrolls, and it took three years to unroll it. When

---

Exodus: An EP Study Commentary, vol. 1 (Darlington, UK: Evangelical Press, 2000), 395–396 n. 24. This idea fits the sense of the name: God is ever-being and ever-acting.

[11] See, for example, Alan H. Gardiner, *Egyptian Grammar*, 3rd ed. (Oxford: Griffith Institute, Ashmolean Museum, 1982), 30.

[12] See Gabriel Barkay, "The Priestly Benediction on the Ketef Hinnom Plaques," *Cathedra* 52 (1989): 37–76 (Hebrew); idem, "The Priestly Benediction on Silver Plaques from Ketef Hinnom in Jerusalem," *Tel Aviv* 19 (1992): 139–192; G. Barkay, A. G. Vaughn, J. Lundberg, and B. Zuckerman, "The Amulets from Ketef Hinnom: A New Edition and Evaluation," *Bulletin of the American Schools of Oriental Research* 334 (2004): 41–71; and Ada Yardeni, "Remarks on the Priestly Blessing on Two Ancient Amulets from Jerusalem," *Vetus Testamentum* 41 (1991): 176–185.

flattened, it measured about three inches long. They noticed that the scroll
was covered with very delicately etched characters. The first word they
were able to decipher was the name "Yahweh" (Hebrew *yhwh*). After much
labor, they were able to read the entire scroll, and it contained the priestly
benediction from Numbers 6. Their translation of it reads:

> YHW . . . the grea[t . . . who keeps] the covenant and [g]raciousness
> toward those who love [him] and (alt: those who love [hi]m) those who
> keep [his commandments . . .] the Eternal? [. . .]. [the?] blessing more
> than any [sna]re and more than Evil. For redemption is in him. For
> YHWH is our restorer [and] rock. May YHWH bles[s] you and [may
> he] keep you. [May] YHWH make [his face] shine . . .[13]

The smaller scroll also contained the priestly benediction from Numbers 6.
It reads as follows:

> [For PN, (the son/daughter of) xxxx] h/hu. May h[e]/sh[e] be blessed by
> YHWH, the warrior [or: helper] and the rebuke of [E]vil; may YHWH
> bless you, keep you. May YHWH make his face shine upon you and
> grant you p[ea]ce.[14]

These passages are the very earliest known citations of biblical texts in
Hebrew.

2. *Kuntillet 'Ajrud inscription.* In the mid-1970s, archaeologists at
the site of Kuntillet 'Ajrud, a settlement in the northern Sinai wilderness,
discovered a collection of Hebrew and Phoenician inscriptions painted
on walls and incised on stone vessels and ceramic storage jars.[15] These
inscriptions are of utmost importance because they contain the names of El
and Yahweh, the common names for God in the Old Testament. They date
to the early eighth century BC and, therefore, predate the Ketef Hinnom
scrolls by at least 150 years.

---

[13] See Barkay, et.al., "Amulets from Ketef Hinnom," 61.
[14] Ibid., 68.
[15] See Ze'ev Meshel, "Did Yahweh Have a Consort? The New Religious Inscriptions from the Sinai," *Biblical Archaeological Review* 5/2 (1979): 24–35; William G. Dever, "Asherah, Consort of Yahweh? New Evidence from Kuntillet 'Ajrud," *Bulletin of the American Schools of Oriental Research* 255 (1984): 21–37; and the first announcement of the finds in S. Singer, "Cache of Hebrew and Phoenician Inscriptions Found in the Desert," *Biblical Archaeological Review* 2/1 (1976): 33–34.

The most spectacular and dramatic discoveries were found on two large *pithoi* or storage jars. One of the *pithoi* contained a drawing that includes three figures: the god Bes, an unidentified deity, and a woman playing a musical instrument. Across the top of the drawing is an inscription that includes the blessing "May you be blessed by Yahweh." On the second *pithoi* is another inscription of blessing, and it reads, ". . . may you be blessed by Yahweh and by his Asherah. Yahweh bless you and keep you and be with you . . ." [16]

The appearance of obvious pagan elements side by side with the name Yahweh is troubling. This syncretism, however, merely reflects the *zeitgeist* or cultural climate of the day. For example, archaeologists discovered a temple complex at the site of Tel Arad that dates to the ninth century BC. The temple was found within the Judean fortress of the site. It appears to be a rogue, syncretistic sanctuary because only the temple in Jerusalem was sanctioned by the Lord. Biblical descriptions of the ninth–eighth centuries BC portray the time as one of common heterodoxy. Jeroboam I (930–910 BC) erected two golden calves in Israel, one in Dan and the other in Bethel. At Bethel, he proclaimed, "Behold, your gods, O Israel, who brought you up out of the land of Egypt" (1 Kings 12:28). Another of Israel's kings, Ahab (874–853 BC), married Jezebel, a Phoenician Baal-worshiper, and she propagated Baal worship throughout Israel.

3. *The Moabite Stone.* According to 2 Samuel 8:2, King David "defeated Moab and he measured them with a line, making them lie down on the ground. Two lines he measured to be put to death, and one full line to be spared. And the Moabites became servants to David and brought tribute." This tributary status apparently lasted through the entire period of the United Monarchy into the reigns of the early kings of the northern kingdom of Israel. The biblical writer tells us that Mesha, king of Moab, brought tribute to Ahab, ruler of Israel (874–853 BC), that consisted of "100,000 lambs and the wool of 100,000 rams" (2 Kings 3:4). Ahab was a strong king who was able to keep Moab under his thumb. His successor, Jehoram (852–841 BC), was much weaker, and consequently Mesha

---

[16] Meshel, "Did Yahweh Have a Consort?" 24–35.

revolted against him (2 Kings 3:5). In order to quell the rebellion, Jehoram mustered the Israelite army, and he appropriated the help of Jehoshaphat, king of Judah, and the king of Edom (2 Kings 3:6–9). This coalition army swept into Moab and had a successful raid; however, in the long run it was not successful, as Israelite hegemony was not reasserted over Moab.

Extrabiblical confirmation of the Moabite rebellion against Israel is extant in the Moabite Stone, discovered in 1868. An inscription on the stone tells of the rebellion from the perspective of Mesha, king of Moab. The text begins with, "I am Mesha, son of Chemosh . . ." The document then describes Mesha's advances and attacks into Israelite-occupied territory. It also tells of Mesha's building projects in towns that he had annexed from Israel. Important for our consideration is the following section of the inscription:

> And Chemosh said to me, "Go, take Nebo from Israel!" So I went by night and fought against it from the break of dawn until noon, taking it and slaying all, seven thousand men, boys, women, girls and maid-servants, for I had devoted them to destruction for (the god) Ashtar-Chemosh. And I took from there the [. . .] of Yahweh, dragging them before Chemosh. And the king of Israel had built Jahaz, and he dwelt there while he was fighting against me, but Chemosh drove him out before me." [17]

This text, and its reference to Yahweh, dates to the mid-ninth century BC. It is, therefore, the oldest extrabiblical text employing the name Yahweh in reference to the God of Israel.

Other texts that employ the name Yahweh ought also to be considered in the discussion before us. I think, in particular, of ostracon number 18 from the Judean site of Arad in the mid-seventh century BC. The author of the text assures his reader that "the house of Yahweh is well; it endures." [18] It is not clear whether the author was referring to the temple in Jerusalem or to the temple that the excavators uncovered at Arad that resembled the temple in Jerusalem. What is certain is that the name Yahweh refers to the God of the Hebrews. The reader also should look at the appearance of the

---

[17] See Pritchard, *Ancient Near Eastern Texts*, 320.
[18] See Yohanan Aharoni, *Arad Inscriptions* (Jerusalem: Israel Exploration Society, 1981); and Dennis Pardee, *Handbook of Ancient Hebrew Letters: A Study Edition* (Chico, CA: Scholars Press, 1982).

name Yahweh at the site of Hamath in northern Syria from the mid- to late eighth century BC. The reason that it appears at this site is unknown and has been a matter of great speculation.[19]

Some historians believe that the earliest extrabiblical document to mention the name Yahweh is a topographical list from the reign of Amenhotep III of the fourteenth century BC. It describes the "land of the Shosu-Yhw." [20] The problem with this text, however, is that the word *Yhw* is being used as a geographical designation, and its connection to the God of Israel is unclear.

The appearance of the epithet "I am that I am" in the Egyptian Book of the Heavenly Cow precedes in time by centuries all of the certain extrabiblical references to the name Yahweh. The irony, of course, is that the Egyptian usage is not in reference to the God of the Hebrews but rather in relation to the chief deity of the Egyptians, the sun-god Re. In the full version of the Book of the Heavenly Cow discovered in the tomb of Seti I (c. 1300 BC), the Pharaoh himself takes on the name *ywy ymy* ("I am who I am"). The transmission of that epithet from Re to Pharaoh is not a problem. The Egyptians believed Pharaoh to be the incarnation of the god Re, and that he is the embodiment of that god signifies that Pharaoh, like Re, is sovereign over all creation.[21]

The Problem and Its Solution

The issue in a nutshell is found in the following question: how are we to understand the use of the divine epithet "I am that I am" in the context of the Egyptian gods? It is certainly common thought that this name was first and uniquely revealed by the God of the Hebrews in the account of the burning bush in Exodus 3, and then uniquely used by him:

> Then Moses said to God, "If I come to the people of Israel and say to them, 'The God of your fathers has sent me to you,' and they ask me, 'What is his name?' what shall I say to them?" God said to Moses, "I AM

---

[19] Stephanie Dalley, "Yahweh in Hamath in the 8th Century B.C.: Cuneiform Materials and Historical Deductions," *Vetus Testamentum* 40 (1990): 23–32; and Ziony Zevit, "Yahweh Worship and Worshippers in 8th Century Syria," *Vetus Testamentum* 41 (1991): 363–366.

[20] Raphael Giveon, *Les Bedouins Shosou des Documents Egyptiens* (Leiden, Netherlands: Brill, 1971).

[21] Pritchard, *Ancient Near Eastern Texts*, 365–367.

WHO I AM." And he said, "Say this to the people of Israel, 'I AM has sent me to you.'" (Ex. 3:13–14)

If this interpretation is correct, how then are we to comprehend the use of this divine epithet for Re, the main god of the Egyptians, and indeed for Pharaoh himself?

In attempting to answer these questions, it is significant that the first time the divine name appears in an extrabiblical text is in an Egyptian document. This certainly fits the context of the God of the Hebrews revealing his covenantal name *yhwh* in his call to Moses to deliver the Israelites out of Egypt. It is doubly significant that the revelation of the name occurs in the context of the most central theme of the book of Exodus: the confrontation between Yahweh and Pharaoh. The true issue at stake in the exodus account is *not* the hostilities between Moses and Pharaoh, or between Moses and the Egyptian magicians, or between Israel and Egypt. What is most important is the contest and battle between Yahweh, the God of Israel, and the Egyptian deities, in particular Re and Pharaoh.

The plague account demonstrates this conflict to a strong degree. Elsewhere I describe the ninth plague upon Egypt in the following manner:

> The ancient Egyptians regarded Amon-Re, the personification of the sun, as their chief deity. They believed that Amon-Re in his rising in the east symbolized new life and resurrection—in fact, they considered him to be the creator-god. Papyrus Boulaq 17 ("Hymn to Amon-Re") reflects the universal reverence the ancient Egyptians paid to the sun-god:
>
>> The goodly beloved youth to whom the gods give praise,
>> Who made what is below and what is above,
>> Who illuminates the Two Lands
>> And crosses the heavens in peace:
>> The King of Upper and Lower Egypt: Ra, the triumphant,
>> Chief of the Two Lands,
>> Great of strength, lord of reverence,
>> The chief one, who made the entire earth.
>> More distinguished than any (other) god . . .[22]

---

[22] Ibid., 365.

But when Amon-Re sank in the west, he represented something different and antithetical: he symbolized death and the underworld. When Yahweh so willed (Ex. 10:21–29), the sun was darkened, and Amon-Re was hidden and unable to shine upon his worshipers. During the ninth plague Amon-Re did not rise again and did not give life; his realm was death, judgment, and hopelessness.[23]

Again, the question at the heart of the book of Exodus is, who is the true God? Who is sovereign over the operation of the universe, and whose will is to come to pass in heaven and on earth? Who is the real "I am that I am"?

The German Egyptologists Hornung and Fecht concluded that the ancient Egyptians borrowed or usurped the divine epithet from the Hebrews, and then applied it to Re and to Pharaoh. These scholars are espousing a rare thing because historians commonly argue that if there are parallels between the Bible and Egypt, it is obvious that the Israelites must have done the borrowing! However, it can easily be demonstrated that cultural practices stream in both directions when two cultures interact. For example, it is likely that the Egyptians under Shoshenk I adapted the structure of Solomon's taxation system to their own administration.[24]

But why would the Egyptians appropriate the name of the God of the Hebrews and apply it to Re and Pharaoh? A staple of Egyptian religious practice was to expropriate the symbols and names of one's enemies as a means of demolishing them. As Alan Gardiner explains, "sometimes it is the hostile power to be destroyed that is counterfeited and done to death." [25] In addition to destruction, the cannibalizing of symbols and names of foes was a means of consuming them and seizing their power. In other words, it was a way of ingesting another's power and character into oneself. In essence, then, Re and Pharaoh's appropriation of the name "I am that I am" was a way to vanquish Yahweh and to abduct his character for themselves. Re and Pharaoh were thus claiming that they were the only eternal, unchanging deities!

Another option is that the Israelites, and indeed God himself, usurped the name from the Egyptians. But why would the Hebrew God take an

[23] Currid, *Ancient Egypt and the Old Testament*, 112.
[24] Ibid., 166.
[25] Alan H. Gardiner, "Magic (Egyptian)," in *Encyclopedia of Religion and Ethics*, ed. James Hastings (Edinburgh: T. & T. Clark, 1908–1926), 8:262–269.

epithet used of Re and Pharaoh and apply it to himself? In reality, such an expropriation was not a unique operation in the Old Testament. For example, the prophet Isaiah announced that "Yahweh is riding on a swift cloud" (19:1). It should be noted that earlier Ugaritic literature used the same epithet for Baal, the storm-god and main god of the Canaanites: "For seven years let Baal fail, eight, the Rider on the Clouds: no dew, no showers, no surging of the two seas, no benefit of Baal's voice" (Aqhat, 42–44).[26] Israel's use of Baal imagery for the work of Yahweh was *not* syncretistic. It was not the merging of the characteristics of two gods into one composite god. Nor was Yahweh somehow evolving from Baal. Rather, Isaiah was making an implicit criticism of Baalism: Baal does not ride on the clouds; only Yahweh does! This was one way in which Isaiah polemicized Canaanite religion; he was taunting that paganism. In addition, the prophet was confirming the truth of Hebrew religion and, in particular, the radical monotheism that it promotes.

The concept of the polemic perhaps was at work in the biblical usage of the divine epithet "I am that I am." The God of Israel employed an originally Egyptian term for Re and Pharaoh to demonstrate that they are not sovereign and all-powerful; they do not run the universe. The name "I am that I am" truly and only belongs to the God of the Hebrews. He uniquely is the eternal, sovereign God of the universe!

Perhaps one might conclude that the divine epithet "I am that I am" in the two cultures was one of simultaneous or near-simultaneous creation. That is unlikely, however, since the Hebrew culture and the Egyptian culture had a long and constant contact with each other, and they often borrowed from one another. Linguistic borrowing was a common feature.[27] Numerous other cultural and religious practices passed between their hands as well.[28] To argue for simultaneous invention of the name in two different but neighboring cultures is improbable at best.

---

[26] Michael D. Coogan, *Stories from Ancient Canaan* (Philadelphia: Westminster, 1978), 41.

[27] See Thomas O. Lambdin, "Egyptian Loan Words in the Old Testament," *Journal of the American Oriental Society* 73 (1953): 145–155; R. J. Williams, "Egypt and Israel," in *The Legacy of Egypt*, ed. John R. Harris, 2nd ed. (Oxford: Clarendon, 1971), 257–290; and idem, "Some Egyptianisms in the Old Testament," in *Studies in Honor of John A. Wilson, Studies in Ancient Oriental Civilizations* 35 (Chicago: University of Chicago, 1969), 93–98.

[28] Scott B. Noegel, "Moses and Magic: Notes on the Book of Exodus," *Journal of the Ancient Near Eastern Society* 24 (1996): 45–59.

So, then, what is the correct answer? To draw the conclusion that the Israelites borrowed the name "I am that I am" from the Egyptians would necessitate a chronology in which Exodus 3 would have been the first use of that epithet in Israel. In the context of the deific contest between Israel's God and the gods of Egypt, the Lord laid down the gauntlet that, in contrast to Pharaoh, he is the only sovereign deity over the universe. That reconstruction appears quite reasonable.

The problem, of course, is that Exodus 3 was not the first revelation of the name Yahweh for the God of the Hebrews. Throughout the book of Genesis he was often referred to by means of the tetragrammaton. The patriarchs, for instance, called him by the name Yahweh within direct speech or dialogue (see Gen. 14:22; 15:8; 28:16, etc.). God, as well, referred to himself by that name (see Gen. 22:16; 28:13, etc.). How, then, are we to explain Moses's ignorance of the name Yahweh in Exodus 3:13, where he said to God, "If I come to the people of Israel and say to them, 'The God of your fathers has sent me to you,' and they ask me, 'What is his name?' what shall I say to them?'"? By asking for God's name, Moses showed that he did not know it. But this does not mean that the name about to be revealed was unknown prior to the burning bush incident. It simply indicates either that the name had somehow been lost to the Hebrews in their many centuries of slavery and contact with paganism, or that it was not a prominent designation for God before the burning bush episode (cf. Ex. 6:2–9).

In light of that reality, it is likely that Hornung and Fecht are correct in their initial assessment that the Egyptians mimicked the Hebrews in the use of the deific formulation "I am that I am." By doing so, the Egyptians were attempting to vanquish and mock the Hebrew God. Re and Pharaoh would then also have ingested the character and traits of the God of the Hebrews. They alone would, therefore, be the sovereign, eternal, and all-powerful deities of the universe.

9

The Rod of Moses

In addition to linguistic parallels utilized as a polemic against Egyptian religion, the Bible records events that were structured as a subtle but powerful critique of Egyptian practice. One such example is the use of a rod or staff by Moses and Aaron in their encounter with Pharaonic Egypt. The element of the "rod" in Exodus has frequently been discussed in the commentaries and elsewhere, yet little attention has been given to the Egyptian background of the rod or staff.[1] I intend to demonstrate the importance of the Egyptian cultural and religious setting to a proper understanding of the rod in the Exodus narratives. In addition, I maintain that this study further supports and confirms the ironic character of the Exodus events and writings.

The Staff in Egypt and in the Bible

The staff or rod was the critical object of the contest between Moses, the representative of Yahweh, and Pharaoh (considered both a god and a high priest of the other gods of Egypt). The Hebrew word used for "staff" by the Exodus writer was *maṭṭeh*, and it was sometimes called *maṭṭeh hā'ĕlōhîm* ("the rod of God") in the narratives.[2] The *maṭṭeh* was princi-

---

[1] Some of the more important commentaries the reader ought to consider include Umberto Cassuto, *A Commentary on the Book of Exodus* (Jerusalem: Magnes, 1983 reprint); Brevard S. Childs, *The Book of Exodus* (Philadelphia: Westminster, 1974); and Martin Noth, *Exodus: A Commentary* (Philadelphia: Westminster, 1962). The earliest attempt to discuss the parallels between rod usage in Egypt and in the Bible was François J. Chabas, "L'Usage des Batons de Main chez les Hebreux et dans L'ancienne Egypte," *Annales du Musee Guimet* 1 (1880): 35–48. Chabas adequately described the purpose of the staff in both cultures, but he does not draw any conclusions based upon parallel usage.

[2] See Exodus 4:20 and 17:9.

pally used in the Bible to refer to a common walking stick (Gen. 38:18, 25). It appears also to have been used as a weapon of defense: the young warrior Jonathan, for example, carried one from battle (1 Sam. 14:27), and Habakkuk employed *maṭṭeh* as a metaphor of God's attack upon evil people (Hab. 3:14). The common expression *maṭṭeh-lĕḥĕm*, "staff of bread" (e.g., Lev. 26:26), probably signified the pole used in carrying bread baskets that is depicted in numerous Egyptian reliefs. That interpretation has been called into question by Mitchell Dahood, although his arguments against it are unconvincing.[3] In any event, the *maṭṭeh-lĕḥĕm* seems to describe a simple, standard agricultural tool or implement of the common Hebrew farmer.

The term *maṭṭeh* appears in the Bible primarily in relation to Egypt. It was not present in the Torah prior to Genesis 38, after Joseph had descended into Egypt. Before that period, the term *maqqēl* was used exclusively for a rod or staff. In addition, of the sixty-three appearances of *maṭṭeh* in the Bible, more than half (thirty-six) concerned Israel's relationship to the land of the Pharaohs.[4]

These concentrated occurrences of *maṭṭeh* make perfectly good sense when one realizes that *maṭṭeh* was probably of Egyptian origin. Alan Gardiner, R. J. Williams, and others have pointed out that it originated from the Egyptian *mdw*, "staff."[5] Although a parallel form, *mṭ yd*, "staff of the hand," was well attested in Ugaritic, apparently it was initially Egyptian.[6] The ancient Egyptians employed various terms for the different types of rods in their culture. Certain words were reserved for the staffs held by deities and royalty, for example. The *ḥk(3)t*, "crook" (?) was the common staff-type used in Egyptian texts and in reliefs that illustrated royal apparel.[7]

---

[3] Mitchell Dahood, in *Psalms III:101–150*, Anchor Bible Commentary (Garden City, NY: Doubleday, 1970), 56, argues that *maṭṭeh-lĕḥĕm* simply means a "stalk of grain."

[4] I include here only the occurrences of *maṭṭeh* that obviously refer to a rod or staff. In Hebrew, the word also served as one of the main words for "tribe." Interestingly, the other principal term for "tribe" is *sebet*, and it also signifies a rod or scepter. The reason that the social structure of the tribe was tied to the words for rod is obvious: each tribe had rods of identification that were different and separate from the other tribes'.

[5] Alan H. Gardiner, *Egyptian Grammar*, 3rd ed. (Oxford: Oxford University Press, 1982), 510; and R. J. Williams, "Egypt and Israel," in *The Legacy of Egypt*, ed. John R. Harris (Oxford: Clarendon, 1971), 263.

[6] *UT* 19:no. 1237; *I Aqht*: 155, 162, 169; and others.

[7] Adolf Erman and Hermann Grapow, *Wörterbuch der ägyptischen Sprache III* (Leipzig: Hinrichs, 1926–1931), 170–173. The word is often translated "scepter" and it was normally part of the *Königswürde* (the king's regalia).

In addition, variations of the word appear as *ḥkȝ* and *ḥkȝt* with a royal determinative, and they signified "rule" and "ruler" respectively. Another standard royal staff was the *nḫḫw*, the "flail, flagellum" (⟋⟍). This was an instrument composed of three long, tapered strips suspended from the end of a whiplike handle.[8] It has been suggested that the *nḫḫw* was originally a shepherd's implement for gathering labdanum, which is a valuable aromatic gum used in perfumes, medicines, and ointments.[9] In consequence, the *nḫḫw* is sometimes referred to as a ladanisterion.[10] The *nḫḫw* was also a standard object of the Pharaonic *Königswürde*. Other scepters and staffs of royalty are well documented from ancient Egypt.[11]

The Egyptian sign for *mdw* (𝖸) merely represented the common walking-stick of the peasantry and of old age.[12] It was the simple ordinary tool of everyday fieldwork; in fact, a variation of *mdw* was used in ancient Egypt to identify the guard or attendant of herds of cattle (*mdw kȝ-ḥd*).[13] That was the type of rod Moses used in the extended confrontation with Pharaoh.

The concept of the "rod of God" was also common in Egypt: it was called the *mdw špśy*, the "holy staff." It was frequently used in reference to the scepters of the gods during the New Kingdom period (c. 1550–1070 BC). Abraham Yahuda comments regarding these objects:

> There were various types of rods for magical purposes, tipped with the heads of various gods and named after them, thus a 'holy rod of Aaron', a 'rod of Khnum', a 'rod of Amon-Ra', a 'rod of Horus of Edfu', a 'rod of Hathor' and many others. Such rods had their special priests and many a high priest had the title, 'the priest of the rod', sometimes with the mention of the god to whose service he was assigned as, for instance, 'a priest of the holy rod of Amon'. Sometimes by the addition

---

[8] William C. Hayes, *The Scepter of Egypt I* (New York: Metropolitan Museum of Art, 1953), 286.

[9] Percy E. Newberry, "The Shepherd's Crook and the So-Called 'Flail' or 'Scourge' of Osiris," *Journal of Egyptian Archaeology* 15 (1929): 84–94.

[10] Labdanum is an exudation on the leaves and shoots of the *gum cistus*, a low shrub that is common in the pasture country of the Near East. By trailing the *nḫḫw* through the foliage, labdanum is collected.

[11] I refer to Gardiner, *Egyptian Grammar*, 508–510. He simply lists the various staff-types and gives a brief explanation of each one.

[12] The *'wt* (𝖸) also symbolized the rod of the peasantry; in fact, the word for "flocks" is related to it. But it was normally replaced in hieroglyphic writing by *nḫḫt*.

[13] Erman and Grapow, *Wörterbuch II*, 178–179. The term also appears in the Egyptian proper name *ns-p -mdw*, "he who belongs to the staff."

of the hieroglyphic sign of a god-determinative the rod was more clearly characterized as divine.[14]

Consequently, the employment of *mdw* and *maṭṭeh* in Egypt and in the biblical narratives was the same. They were both used in the context of the common, everyday life of the herdsman, as an instrument of travel, and as a symbol of the power of a deity.

The Symbol of the Rod in Ancient Egypt

The staff of Pharaoh in ancient Egypt was emblematic of royalty, power, and authority.[15] The rod as a symbol of Pharaonic sovereignty began at the coronation of the king, when the crook was placed in his hand. Pyramid Texts 196–203 describe that scene of enthronement as follows:

> Stand (as king) over it, over this land which has come forth from Atum,
> The spittle which has come forth from the beetle.[a]
> Be (king) over it; be high over it,
> That thy father may see thee,
> That he may see thee.
> He comes to thee, O father of his;
> He comes to thee, O Re . . .
> Let him grasp the Heavens
> And receive the Horizon;
> Let him dominate the Nine Bows[b]
> And equip (with offerings) the Ennead.[c]
> Give the crook into his hand.
> So that the head of Lower and Upper Egypt shall be bowed.

[a] The dung-beetle was a representation of the god Re in his early rising from the underworld. It, therefore, meant new life and resurrection.

[b] The Egyptian name commonly used for foreign lands.

[c] The term refers to the nine gods of Heliopolis that symbolized the order of creation in society.[16]

---

[14] Abraham S. Yahuda, *The Accuracy of the Bible* (London: William Heinemann, 1934), 106–107. Admittedly, one must be careful when citing Yahuda's work because he frequently overstates his case. In this instance, I would suggest that his description of the holy rod in Egypt is essentially correct.

[15] Chabas, in "L'Usage des Batons," says that rods throughout the ancient Near East had a metaphorical purpose, primarily as insignia of dignity and authority (p. 35).

[16] Henri Frankfort, *Kingship and the Gods* (Chicago: University of Chicago Press, 1948), 109.

The presentation of the rod at coronation signified the transference of power from above to the new Pharaoh. The crook was simply the repository of the deific force of royalty.

After the coronation, the royal staff belonged to the ceremonial insignia of the Egyptian king. In reliefs and sculptures from all periods the Pharaoh was pictured holding some type of staff. Examples are legion. Important Pharaohs like Pepi I (Old Kingdom), Senusret I (Middle Kingdom), Akhenaten, Tutankhamen, Ramses II, and Horemhab (New Kingdom), and others were often portrayed bearing a royal staff.[17] Egyptian literature also habitually mentioned the royal staff when speaking of the kings of Egypt.[18] The rod was also the symbol of the authority and power of the gods (called the *mdw nṯr*, "rod of god"). In Egyptian reliefs and on statues the gods were pictured carrying staffs in their hands. In the tomb of Pharaoh Horemhab of the Eighteenth Dynasty (c. 1319–1307 BC), for instance, there is a relief showing the king presenting gifts and adorations to Hathor, "the lady of the gods," and to Harsiese, "the King of gods." [19] Both deities are holding shepherd's crooks in their palms. In the double scene of the lintel of Senusret III (c. 1878–1841 BC) at Nag' el-Madamud, the king is giving offerings to Montu, "Lord of Thebes," who is bearing a staff in his hand.[20] Many more references could easily be cited.

The shepherd's staff as an emblem of the authority of the gods was an early Egyptian belief and custom. It appeared as far back as the Early Pre-Dynastic period as a symbol of the authority of 'Andjety, the god of a transient shepherd people who wandered in the district of Busiris (Abusir) in the central Delta.[21] 'Andjety soon disappeared as an important deity in Egypt, but through the common process of assimilation the god Osiris adopted some of the iconographic attributes of 'Andjety. The crook became one of the most significant characteristics of Osiris beginning in the Late Predynastic period and continuing throughout the dynastic ages.

[17] See Kazimierz Michalowski, *The Art of Ancient Egypt* (New York: Abrams, 1970), 91, 208, and 254–255.
[18] James H. Breasted, *Ancient Records of Egypt I-IV* (Chicago: University of Chicago Press, 1906), I:136; II:406; III:8.
[19] John Baines and Jaromir Malek, *Atlas of Ancient Egypt* (New York: Facts on File, 1980), 100.
[20] Ibid., 110.
[21] Hayes, *Scepter of Egypt I*, 268.

Osiris, of course, rose to the level of universal deity in Egypt. He was king of the underworld and conqueror of death, and he embodied the Egyptian conception of kingship. Numerous symbols were associated with the cult of Osiris, such as the white crown with plumes, and mummification—but no tokens were as prominent as the shepherd's crook and the flagellum. They simply signified all of Osiris's power, authority, and sovereignty. The rods were so identified with Osiris that ancient Egyptian literature referred to him as the *sekhem-sceptre*, "power of the rod." [22]

The Pharaohs of Egypt desired to be identified with Osiris because they were then assured of attaining the resurrection. As Frankfort points out, "all kings survived in the Beyond as Osiris." [23] In addition, while reigning on earth, Egyptian kings wanted to be endowed with the divine right of Osiris: they sought the investment of his dominion, force, and omnipotence. Thus, the Pharaohs carried the shepherd's crook and the flagellum as emblems of their identification with Osiris and their having received his authority and power.

The Magical Staff

The scepter of Pharaoh was, however, more than a mere symbol of suzerainty. The ancient Egyptians truly believed that the royal staff was imbued with magic and the power of the gods. The idea that inanimate objects could be charged with power—the power of the gods—was always foundational to Egyptian religion. The various crowns of royalty, for example, were considered sacred objects in possession of divine powers. Even temple furniture was venerated as a great god.[24] Not only were physical objects considered to be charged with divine potency, but the very name of a person or thing was believed to bear deific force.[25] In support of Egyptian royal staffs having been endued with deific character was the fact that the hieroglyphic sign of a god-determinative often accompanied the word for "rod."

---

[22] Jaroslav Cerny, *Ancient Egyptian Religion* (Westport, CT: Greenwood, 1957), 59.

[23] Frankfort, *Kingship and the Gods*, 197.

[24] Adolf Erman, *A Handbook of Egyptian Religion* (London: Constable, 1907), 75.

[25] See "The God and His Unknown Name of Power," in *Ancient Near Eastern Texts Relating to the Old Testament*, ed. James B. Pritchard, 3rd ed. (Princeton, NJ: Princeton University Press, 1969), 12–14. The story tells of Re having a hidden name which was a source of his power. Isis plots to learn the name so that she can secure power for herself.

The magicians of Egypt (*hry-ḥbt*) also carried staffs in order to perform their magical feats. It is recorded that when attacked by enemies, the magician-king Nectanebo II (c. 360–343 BC) turned wax figures of soldiers and ships into an animate force by means of a magical rod. Numerous scarabs attest to that practice by containing scenes of magicians holding rods in their hands that could instantly be turned into snakes.[26] Wallis Budge claims that the practice of rod divination operated among the magicians of Egypt and refers to "from time immemorial . . . a wonderful rod of which they worked wonders."[27] Just as with the royal staffs, the Egyptians believed the magicians' rods to be charged with superhuman strength. The magicians were thus invested with mysterious magical forces of the gods personified in the rods. The crooks simply gave them divine *ḥkꜣ*, "magical power."

The Irony of the Rod in the Exodus Account

When Moses and Aaron confronted Pharaoh in Exodus 5–14, they were in possession of a rod by which they performed many signal wonders. With that staff they brought on Egypt numerous plagues, and eventually they used it to destroy the Egyptian army in the Red Sea (Ex. 14:16). The use of a rod to perform all those disastrous feats was a physical example of judicial irony. It was simply an extensive polemic against Egyptian culture and belief. As we have seen, the ancient Egyptians understood that a staff was a symbol of authority, leadership, and power. The irony of the matter is that the two Hebrew leaders possessed a rod, a highly esteemed Egyptian emblem, in order to humiliate and defeat the Egyptians. That is to say, the very physical symbol that rendered glory to Egypt, authority to Egypt, power to Egypt, was the very object the Hebrews used to vanquish them. Hengstenberg comments, "Moses was furnished with power to perform that which the Egyptian magicians most especially gloried in, and by which they most of all supported their authority."[28]

---

[26] For examples of these scarabs, see Louis Keimer, *Histoires des Serpents dans l'Égypte ancienne et moderne* (Mémoires, Institut d'Égypte 50, 1947), 16–17, figs. 14–21. A scarab is a sculpted representation of a dung beetle.

[27] E. A. Wallis Budge, *Egyptian Magic* (New Hyde Park, NY: University Books, 1958 reprint), 5.

[28] Ernst W. Hengstenberg, *Egypt and the Books of Moses* (Edinburgh: Thomas Clark, 1845), 98.

With rod in hand, the two Hebrews were also proclaiming a deific rivalry between the gods of Egypt and Yahweh, the God of Israel. As shown above, the magical powers of the gods, especially Osiris, were personified in the holy rods of Egypt. Pharaoh and the magicians of Egypt, possessors of the holy rods, were thought to be particularly superhuman because of those imputed powers. Again, the symbol of that invested power of the gods was the rod. When Moses first used his crook and flung it before Pharaoh and the lector-priests, he was assaulting that token of deific authority and power.[29] Moses was announcing the power imbued in his shepherd's staff to be far greater and far more efficacious than that of the Egyptian rods. Indeed, when Aaron's rod swallowed the staffs of the Egyptian magicians, it was a sign of Yahweh's omnipotence, and it was an outright rejection and conquering of the *ḥkз*, the "magical power" of the gods, in their Egyptian staffs.[30] The staffs of Pharaoh and the magicians had no power against Yahweh. Their force was absent in the face of the might of the Hebrew God endowed in the *maṭṭeh hā'ĕlōhîm*.

The preceding point defines for us the true issue at stake in the Exodus event: it demonstrates that the hostilities were not primarily between Moses and Pharaoh, or between Moses and the Egyptian magicians, or for that matter, between Israel and Egypt. What the rod confrontation portrays is

> . . . a heavenly combat—a war between the God of the Hebrews and the deities of Egypt. For the biblical writer, the whole episode of Israel in Egypt was a matter of theology. It was a question of who was the one true God, who was sovereign over the operation of the universe, and whose will was to come to pass in heaven and upon earth.[31]

The rod conflict introduces us to that drama in grand theological form: Yahweh, God of Israel, engages the gods of Egypt in a contest of power and will.

---

[29] John D. Currid, "The Egyptian Setting of the 'Serpent' Confrontation in Exodus 7:8–13," *Biblische Zeitschrift* 39/2 (1995): 215 n. 56.

[30] It is important to note that Exodus 7:12 does not say that Aaron's snake swallowed the Egyptian snakes, but that his rod swallowed their rods. The point is that the rod was a symbol of authority, power, and sovereignty, and it was that emblem that was vanquished by Yahweh.

[31] Currid, "Egyptian Setting," 206.

Finally, it is ironic that Moses employed a simple shepherd's crook in the conflict with Egypt. He did not engage Pharaoh with a mighty, elaborate scepter of Egyptian royalty—the *ḥk3t* or the *nḫḫw*—but he came with the common *mdw* of the herder. According to the biblical author, the Egyptians clearly despised the lowly occupation of shepherding: Joseph is portrayed as separating the Hebrews from the Egyptians in Genesis 46 "because every shepherd is loathsome to the Egyptians" (v. 34b, AT). Moses's use of the *mdw* would have been insulting to Egyptian royalty and priesthood. How could a mere shepherd's staff match up with the royal staffs endowed with the power of Osiris? That idea underscores the theology of the Exodus writer that the real power of the universe was not in the staff but in the god. Yahweh was victorious, not because of the type of rod that was used, but by his great power and sovereignty. That is the main message of the Exodus account.

Conclusion

The Egyptian background of the rod in the Exodus narratives ought to impress on our minds the realistic character of the events of the exodus. The writer was quite knowledgeable of Egyptian culture and religion. In order to criticize Egyptian practices and to demonstrate the truth of the Hebrew religion, he used that detailed understanding in a subtle but powerful way. He simply polemicized Egyptian beliefs in order to exalt Yahweh as the true sovereign of the universe. That was accomplished not only by employing linguistic parallels but also by structuring the very events and objects of the episode as a critique of Egyptian practice. What a masterful, skillful, and profound way to argue! It truly stands as a monument to the literary genius of the Exodus author.

10

The Parting of the Waters of the Red Sea

The Red Sea crossing, recorded in Exodus 14:13–31, is the salient event in the history of Israel. More than any other historical incident, it left a lasting and striking impression upon later biblical writers (see Ps. 78:13; 106:9–10; Isa. 50:2; 51:10; 63:12). God's salvation of Israel at the sea was so important that it came to be portrayed as a paradigm for later events of deliverance in the life of Israel, such as the return from Babylonian captivity (e.g., Zech. 10:10–11). It is simply the great event of God's deliverance of his people in the Old Testament. For example, at the very heart of Psalm 136, the biblical author says:

> to him who struck down the firstborn of Egypt,
> > for his steadfast love endures forever;
> and brought Israel out from among them,
> > for his steadfast love endures forever;
> with a strong hand and an outstretched arm,
> > for his steadfast love endures forever;
> to him who divided the Red Sea in two,
> > for his steadfast love endures forever;
> and made Israel pass through the midst of it,
> > for his steadfast love endures forever;
> but he overthrew Pharaoh and his host in the Red Sea,
> > for his steadfast love endures forever. (vv. 10–15)

Thus, in Scripture, the parting of the Red Sea is a singular, prominent, and extraordinary event in the history of God's redemptive work.

It is intriguing and important for us to note that the ancient Egyptians, in fact, had their own account of how a priest separated a large body of water. The story is a part of the Westcar Papyrus (also known as "King Cheops and the Magicians"), named after its discoverer, Henry Westcar. It contains twelve rolls of papyrus and is currently on display in the Egyptian section of the Berlin Museum.[1] We will now take some time to consider the contents of this document, and then we will attempt to discern if it has any relationship to the biblical account of the Red Sea crossing.

The Westcar Papyrus

CONTENT

This cycle of stories focuses on the miracles of magicians or lector-priests during the Third and Fourth Dynasties of ancient Egypt (c. 2649–2465 BC). Cheops (Khufu), builder of the Great Pyramid at Giza, asks his sons to tell him stories of the feats of magicians as a form of amusement and pleasure. The tales are simple, short, and in chronological order. The manuscript is only partially preserved because most of the opening tale is missing and the end of the document is abruptly cut off. Precisely how much of the papyrus is missing is unknown.

Since only the ending of Tale One is preserved, it is uncertain which son of Cheops narrated it. What remains of the story relates an event during the time of Djoser, who built the Step Pyramid at Saqqara (2630–2611 BC). It tells of payment being made to a lector-priest as a result of his work and wisdom. Some would argue that perhaps this magician was the famous Egyptian official Imhotep, but this is mere speculation.[2] The Second Tale is told by Khafre (Chephren), who was the builder of the second pyramid at Giza. The setting of his story is the reign of Nebka in the Third

---

[1] The literature discussing the Westcar Papyrus is vast. A good starting place for readers interested in this text is the following: A. M. Blackman, *The Story of King Kheops and the Magicians* (Reading, UK: J. V. Books, 1988); Miriam Lichtheim, *The Old and Middle Kingdoms*, vol. 1 of *Ancient Egyptian Literature* (Berkeley: University of California Press, 1975), 215–222; and R. B. Parkinson, *The Tale of Sinuhe and Other Egyptian Poems 1940–1640 B.C.* (Oxford: Oxford University Press, 1997), 102–107.

[2] William K. Simpson, ed., *The Literature of Ancient Egypt*, 3rd ed. (New Haven, CT: Yale University Press, 2003), 14 n. 1.

Dynasty. He describes a tale of a lector-priest named Webaoner who fashions a crocodile out of wax and turns it into a real animal.[3] This story is truly reminiscent of the similar feat of Moses when he turns his staff into a serpent and then turns the serpent back into a rod (Ex. 4:1–5). Cheops's third son, Bauefre, relates the Third Tale, and it contains a story of a lector-priest during the reign of Snefru (c. 2575–2551 BC). The content of this episode is the salient material for our discussion in this chapter, and thus it will be dealt with in detail below. The Fourth Tale is contemporary to the time of Cheops, and it is told by his son Hardedef. Hardedef himself plays an important role in the story, which concerns a marvel performed by a man named Dedi. The latter is a mythic figure for certain, since Hardedef describes him as "a townsman of 110 years, and he eats 500 loaves, a shoulder of beef as meat, and as drink 100 jugs to this day. He knows how to reattach a head which has been cut off. . ."[4] The Fifth Tale is a prophecy of Cheops's line of descent, ending with the birth of three kings who are the first kings of the Fifth Dynasty: Userkaf (c. 2465–2458), Sahure (c. 2458–2446), and Kakai (c. 2446–2426).

DATE

The Westcar Papyrus is a single document that was inscribed in the Eighteenth Dynasty (c. 1550–1307 BC).[5] However, the original composition is probably earlier, perhaps from the Twelfth Dynasty (c. 1991–1783 BC). It purports to describe events that occurred in the Third–Fourth Dynasties; the document, therefore, was written some 500–600 years after the events it describes.

PURPOSE

The Westcar Papyrus was "not intended to be a historically reliable document," and it was "not written as conscientious history."[6] It is, in reality,

---

[3] See chapter 2 above, where we discuss this story in greater detail.

[4] Simpson, *Literature of Ancient Egypt*, 18.

[5] There is some disagreement regarding the dating of the extant manuscript. Georges Posener believes it actually was written during the Second Intermediate/Hyksos Period (c. 1640–1532 BC). See the discussion in John R. Harris, ed., *The Legacy of Egypt*, 2nd ed. (Oxford: Clarendon, 1971), 237.

[6] Harold M. Hays, "The Historicity of Papyrus Westcar," *Zeitschrift für Ägyptische Sprache und Altertumskunde* 129 (2002): 20–30.

an example of an attempt to historicize mythology. The text itself is pro-pagandistic, that is, it is a fictional account used in an ideological fash-ion. Egyptian writers often rely heavily on myth to promote succession of kingship.[7] The point of the Westcar Papyrus appears to be the political legitimization of the contemporary kingship of the Twelfth Dynasty in contrast to earlier Pharaohs. As Harold Hays comments, "the point of the text emerges from the contrast drawn between the old line, frivolous and self-serving, and a new line, serious and properly in service to the gods." [8] The text is therefore a good example of *encomium* (formal expression of praise) for present royalty at the expense of earlier kingship.

THE THIRD TALE

Bauefre, the third son of Cheops, tells the king of a marvelous incident that had taken place during the reign of Snefru in the Fourth Dynasty. Snefru was the father of Cheops, and the son had directly succeeded his father to the throne of Egypt. The story is about King Snefru searching the palace to find the chief lector-priest, named Djadjaemonkh. The monarch is bored, and so he wants counsel on how to find some pleasure. Djadjaemonkh suggests the following:

> Let your majesty proceed to the lake of the palace, l.p.h.,[9] and equip for yourself a boat with all the beauties who are in your palace chamber. The heart of Your Majesty shall be refreshed at the sight of their rowing as they row up and down. You can see the beautiful fish pools of your lake, and you can see its beautiful fields around it. Your heart will be refreshed at this.[10]

The king takes the advice of the lector-priest, and he is happy and content with the outing.

A problem interrupts his pleasure, however, as one of the rowers drops her turquoise, fish-shaped charm into the water. She will accept no sub-

---

[7] John Van Seters, *In Search of History: Historiography in the Ancient World and the Origins of Biblical History* (New Haven, CT: Yale University Press, 1983), 181.
[8] Hays, "Historicity of Papyrus Westcar," 29.
[9] An epithetic formula which often appears in reference to Egyptian royalty; it is an abbreviation that means "Life, prosperity, health."
[10] Simpson, *Literature of Ancient Egypt*, 16.

stitute, so Snefru calls for Djadjaemonkh to solve the problem with his secret arts. The tale unfolds as follows:

> Then said the chief lector Djadjaemonkh his magic sayings. He placed one side of the water of the lake upon the other, and lying upon a potsherd he found the fish-shaped charm. Then he brought it back and it was given to its owner. Now as for the water, it was twelve cubits deep, and it amounted to twenty-four cubits after it was folded back.[11] He said his magic sayings, and he brought back the water of the lake to its position. His Majesty passed holiday with the entire palace, l.p.h. When he came forth, he rewarded the chief lector Djadjaemonkh with all good things.[12]

Djadjaemonkh thus divides the lake and then brings the water of the lake back to its original position and depth by means of his magical sayings.

The Red Sea

The Third Tale of the Westcar Papyrus is reminiscent of the biblical account of Israel's crossing of the Red Sea, recorded in Exodus 14. R. J. Williams comments, "It is possible that the account of Moses's dramatic division of the waters of the Sea of Reeds (Ex. 14:21f.) owes its inspiration to the similar feat of the ancient Egyptian magician Djadjaemonekh as related in the Westcar Papyrus." [13] The similarities between the two stories are evident: the two religious, spiritual leaders divide a deep body of water through supernatural means. The chief lector-priest of Egypt accomplishes his separation through his magical arts and sayings; the Hebrew prophet does the same thing by means of a rod empowered by the deity Yahweh (Ex. 14:15–18). Both leaders are successful in their work of separating the waters, and they are both able to return the waters to their original position (Ex. 14:27).

Because the Hebrew account of the crossing of the Red Sea was written later than the story of King Cheops and the magicians, one wonders if

---

[11] If this is the royal Egyptian cubit, then it measures approximately 20 inches in length. The lake is thus about 20 feet deep.

[12] Quoted in Simpson, *Literature of Ancient Egypt*, 17–18.

[13] Quoted in Harris, *Legacy of Egypt*, 271.

and how the biblical writer may be using the parallel. A major distinction between the two pieces is that the Egyptian story is obviously not meant to be taken as historical literature, whereas the Hebrew writer clearly intended his material to be regarded as historical fact. The Egyptian account is myth; the Hebrew account is not. In this book I adopt the classic understanding of mythology that has been presented by Paul Veyne and others.[14] This view would say, for example, in regard to the Greek myth of Theseus, the purported founder-king of Athens, that the Greeks knew he never slew the Minotaur. Yet they were still capable of believing in the existence of Theseus, of creating a genealogy for him, and assigning to him numerous historical deeds. This is a process of contradiction, in which history is applied to myth even though such events never really took place. Ancient myth is thus the created history of the imagination. To the contrary, the Hebrew account of the exodus out of Egypt was written as historical narrative, and as a factual presentation of events that truly happened in time and space. In this sense, the historical narrative of the Israelites is radically anti-mythic, and in no manner or way is it fanciful.

It seems clear that the biblical writer regarded the event of the crossing of the Red Sea as a polemical parallel with the myth of Djadjaemonkh's separation of the waters of the lake. The chief lector-priest of Egypt may have divided a lake in search of a valuable charm, but the God of the Hebrews, through Moses, parts the entire Red Sea and causes a nation to pass through on dry ground. What was mythic in Egyptian literature has become real and factual in time and history as recorded by the biblical writer. And this parallel is polemical because it highlights and accentuates the work of Yahweh that was done in history over against what was merely accomplished in the imagination of the Egyptian writer.

Polemics in the Red Sea Account

The episode of the parting of the Red Sea contains other polemical elements that indicate that the taunting of Egypt by the biblical writer is an

---

[14] Paul Veyne, *Did the Greeks Believe in Their Myths? An Essay on Constitutive Imagination*, trans. Paula Wissing (Chicago: University of Chicago Press, 1988).

important aspect of the account. In fact, the entire exodus event itself includes a polemical twist. This is hardly surprising. During the eighth plague on Egypt, God gives the Israelites two reasons that he is delivering his people out of Egypt. The text says he is doing this so "that you may tell in the hearing of your son and of your grandson how I have dealt harshly with the Egyptians and what signs I have done among them, that you may know that I am the LORD" (Ex. 10:2). The first reason for the exodus is to educate the Israelites and their posterity regarding the person and work of Yahweh. The second purpose is as a judgment against Egypt. The verb "to deal harshly" is in a Hebrew verbal stem that bears a sense of mockery. Brown, Driver, and Briggs appropriately translate this clause as "how I have made a toy of Egypt." [15] Yahweh not only brings judgment on the Egyptians, but he taunts them in the process. At this point I will provide several examples of polemics in the Red Sea account.

THE EGYPTIAN DEITY AMON-RE

The ancient Egyptians regarded Amon-Re, the personification of the sun, as their chief deity. They believed that the sun-god is born anew each morning in its rising in the east, and this daily activity symbolizes new life and resurrection. They held Amon-Re in the highest esteem, and their reverence for him is demonstrated in Papyrus Boulaq 17 (often called "The Hymn to Amon-Re"). As we have seen, this text says about the sun-god,

> The goodly beloved youth to whom the gods give praise,
> Who made what is below and what is above,
> Who illuminates the Two Lands
> And crosses the heavens in peace:
> The King of Upper and Lower Egypt: Ra, the triumphant,
> Chief of the Two Lands,
> Great of strength, lord of reverence,
> The chief one, who made the entire earth.
> More distinguished than any (other) god . . .[16]

---

[15] F. Brown, S. R. Driver, and C. A. Briggs, *A Hebrew and English Lexicon of the Old Testament* (Oxford: Oxford University Press, 1929), 759. In 1 Samuel 6:6 this same verb is used again of God mocking the Egyptians.
[16] James B. Pritchard, ed., *Ancient Near Eastern Texts Relating to the Old Testament*, 2nd ed. (Princeton, NJ: Princeton University Press, 1955), 365.

As the sun-god rises in the east, "the whole creation rejoices, and he may be greeted by gods and goddesses, the king, the 'eastern souls,' personifications of categories of humanity, and baboons that screech acclamation." [17]

After his birth in the east, the sun-god then crosses the sky in a solar bark, ages, and dies as he sets in the west. He travels through the underworld at night before being born again at daybreak. As Amon-Re sinks in the west he symbolizes death, darkness, and the underworld.

Just prior to the dividing of the Red Sea, we read that the pillar of cloud separated the army of Egypt and the people of Israel, who were standing by the sea. The text literally says, "And it came between the camp of Egypt and the camp of Israel. And there was the cloud with the darkness and it gave light to the night. And one did not come near the other all night" (Ex. 14:20, AT). A good and proper interpretation of this verse is that one side of the cloud brought light and the other side gave darkness. The Egyptians were clothed in darkness, and the Hebrews were bathed in light. Amon-Re and Pharaoh, the incarnation of the sun-god, could not bring light to their people. The Egyptian army remained in darkness, and this symbolized judgment and death upon them.

This scene is reminiscent of the ninth plague, in which Yahweh willed Egypt to be in darkness. Consequently Amon-Re was hidden and unable to shine upon his worshipers (Ex. 10:21–29). During that plague Amon-Re did not rise again and did not give life; his realm was death, judgment, and hopelessness.

In general, the Israelite authors were quite familiar with the cult of Re in Egypt. "In certain pentateuchal texts, for example, the biblical author employed obvious wordplays on the name of the Egyptian god Re/Ra and the Hebrew concept of *ra'* ("evil"). Apparent allusions are found in Exodus 5:19; 10:10; 32:12, 22; Numbers 11:1; 20:5; and Deuteronomy 9:18. These double entendres were for the purpose of ridiculing the chief deity of Egypt." [18]

---

[17] John Baines and Jaromir Malek, *Atlas of Ancient Egypt* (New York: Facts on File, 1990 reprint), 216.

[18] John D. Currid, *Ancient Egypt and the Old Testament* (Grand Rapids, MI: Baker, 1997), 112–113. For an important discussion of these wordplays, see Gary A. Rendsburg, "The Egyptian Sun-God Ra in the Pentateuch," *Henoch* 10 (1988): 3–15.

THE ACT OF SWALLOWING

One of the consequences of the episode of the parting of the sea is that "the earth swallowed" the Egyptian army. In Egyptian culture, the act of swallowing was one of great magical importance and significance.[19] According to Robert Ritner, "Consumption entails the absorption of an object and the acquisition of its benefits or traits. Alternatively, the act can serve a principally hostile function, whereby 'devour' signifies 'to destroy'— though even here the concept of acquiring power may be retained." [20] Also, in Egyptian magical texts the term "to swallow" means "to know" and to have power over an object or a person.[21] Therefore, when God had the Red Sea "swallow" the Egyptian army, it was destroying not only the Egyptian forces: the language of the biblical text reflects also absorption of their power, authority, and knowledge.

HARDENING OF THE HEART

During the event of the crossing of the Red Sea, Yahweh explains to the Israelites one of the major purposes for his acting on their behalf: "And I will harden Pharaoh's heart, and he will pursue them, and I will get glory over Pharaoh and all his host, and the Egyptians shall know that I am the LORD" (Ex. 14:4). The hardening of Pharaoh's heart is a principal motif in the exodus account (see, for instance, Ex. 4:21; 7:3; 9:12; 10:1, 20, 27; 14:8). I have tried to demonstrate elsewhere that the theme of the "hardening of Pharaoh's heart" is a polemical play against the prevailing Egyptian belief in the pure and untainted character of Pharaoh. I will not repeat the arguments here but will point the reader to the relevant literature.[22]

---

[19] Scott B. Noegel, "Moses and Magic: Notes on the Book of Exodus," *Journal of the Ancient Near Eastern Society* 24 (1996): 45–59.

[20] Robert K. Ritner, *The Mechanics of Ancient Egyptian Magical Practice*, Studies of Ancient Oriental Civilization 54 (Chicago: Oriental Institute, 1993), 103.

[21] Noegel, "Moses and Magic," 49.

[22] See John D. Currid, "Why Did God Harden Pharaoh's Heart?" *Bible Review* 9/6 (1993): 46–51; idem, "The Egyptian Setting of the Serpent Confrontation," *Biblische Zeitschrift* 204/4 (1991): 18–40; idem, *Ancient Egypt and the Old Testament*, 96–103.

11

Canaanite Motifs

Michael Coogan, in his translation and commentary of some of the myths of the Canaanites, makes the following intriguing statement:

> Canaanite motifs are ubiquitous in the Bible. Most significant is the fu-
> sion of Baal-language and El-language in the descriptions of Yahweh
> and his activity: the god of Israel may be unique, but the formulae with
> which Israel expressed her understanding of him were not. The more we
> learn of the cultural context in which the Israelites lived, the more the
> prophetic mark rings true: By origin and by birth you are of the land of
> the Canaanites. (Ezekiel 16:3).[1]

Coogan is certainly correct about one thing: there are numerous parallels
in themes and details between Canaanite texts and the biblical accounts.
On the other hand, the reason he gives to account for these many parallels
is questionable. He appears to be saying that the Hebrew writers merely
borrowed numerous Canaanite motifs of theology and applied them to
Yahweh, with minimal discrimination, for, in reality, Israelites were probably Canaanites originally. Thus, if I read Coogan correctly, Yahweh is
actually not all that unique as a deity, in light of parallels and borrowings
that Israel indiscriminately took from Canaanite literature.

Is that the only way to understand the parallel figures used of the Canaanite pantheon and Yahweh? Is this relationship mere borrowing? Is it

---

[1] Michael D. Coogan, *Stories from Ancient Canaan* (Philadelphia: Westminster, 1978), 23.

mere syncretism? Are the Hebrew writers simply guilty of plagiarism and of then cleansing the pagan elements from their theology? Or, perhaps, the relationship between the two is much more complicated than the Hebrew writers simply pirating Canaanite motifs and using them for their own Yahwistic purposes. To begin to understand the complexity of that relationship, let's begin our study with a brief overview of Canaanite literature, that is, its provenance, date, and basic content.

Literature from Canaan

The vast majority of ancient Canaanite texts come from the site of Ugarit (often referred to as Ras Shamra), on the north Syrian coast along the Mediterranean Sea. Ugarit was a prominent Canaanite city-state during the second millennium BC. Excavations began at the site in 1929, and they have continued almost uninterrupted into the twenty-first century, except for a hiatus during the decade around World War II (1939–1948). A most important find at Ras Shamra/Ugarit was hundreds of texts discovered in the palace and temple areas of the site. Olof Pedersen has determined that seventeen archives of texts have been uncovered at the site, and more than 1,500 of these tablets have been published.[2] A small number of Canaanite texts come from other sites in the Levant (such as Syria and Israel), but most of them have been found at Ugarit.

Ugarit was at its politico-socioeconomic height in the fifteenth–thirteenth centuries BC. This is the time when the written literature began to flourish; it is the golden age of the literary life of the site. Ugarit met its final fate by being destroyed around 1200 BC, presumably by the "Sea Peoples," various groups of invaders from the general area of Greece and the Aegean islands.

The Ugaritic texts feature a variety of writing styles: "They include diplomatic correspondence, legal records, remedies for horses' ailments, long lists of gods, offerings, supplies, and personnel, dictionaries of word equivalents in the various languages used in the city, and the oldest com-

---

[2] Olof Pedersen, *Archives and Libraries in the Ancient Near East 1500–300 B.C.* (Bethesda, MD: Capital Decisions, 1998), 70–74.

plete alphabet, with an order substantially the same as that of our own." [3]
The best preserved and most well-known literary texts from the site are
the Baal Cycle, the Legend of Aqhat, and the Legend of Keret. The famous
scribe Ilimilku is known to have copied, transcribed, and collated several
of the literary works. William Schniedewind and Joel Hunt are correct
when they comment, "This literature has opened a window into the culture
of the late second millennium and has supplied a surprising treasure of
cultural, religious, and linguistic insight into ancient Israel." [4]

The specific literary texts just mentioned were all discovered in the
library of the chief priest of Baal in the main temple complex of the
city. These texts, along with subsidiary texts found elsewhere on the
site, provide the basic myths upon which our knowledge of Ugaritic
religion is founded. In turn, these texts help us understand the religious
context of the Old Testament, and we can see many parallels between
Canaanite and Israelite religious practices. Our aim in this chapter is to
try to glean some insight into the relationship between the two, and so
we will begin with a brief description of Canaanite theology as found in
the Ugaritic texts.

The Canaanite Pantheon

The head of the pantheon according to the Ugaritic texts was the god El.
He was ruler of the gods and the cosmos, as his epithets "father of the
gods" and "king" bear witness. The name El is a common one throughout
the ancient Near East that simply means "god." Its etymology is debated,
although it likely derives from a Semitic word that means "strength." Ugaritic myth locates El's home on the top of a mountain from which two rivers proceed that provide all the water on earth; his home is "in the midst
of the headwaters of the Two Oceans." [5] There El lived in a tent, and the
divine assembly of the gods met at that place under his rule and authority.

A second tier of gods is called the "Assembled Body" in the Baal-

---

[3] Coogan, *Stories from Ancient Canaan*, 10.
[4] William M. Schniedewind and Joel H. Hunt, *A Primer on Ugaritic: Language, Culture, and Literature* (Cambridge: Cambridge University Press, 2007), 21.
[5] Quoted in James B. Pritchard, ed., *Ancient Near Eastern Texts Relating to the Old Testament*, 2nd ed. (Princeton, NJ: Princeton University Press, 1955), 129.

Anath myth.[6] These numerous gods were personified in various elements of nature. Baal, for example, was the storm-god, and his consort Anath was the goddess of love and war. Baal's adversary was Mot, who was the god of death and the underworld. Baal's father was Dagon, the god of agriculture. In the texts there is also a third tier of gods, who were employed as servants to the other deities.

In some of the Ugaritic writings, such as the Baal Cycle, the god Baal seems to have superseded El as the most powerful and central god of the pantheon. Baal even claimed, "I alone will rule over the gods," and the cycle narrates the story of Baal's rise to supreme power by his defeating the forces of chaos. Baal, like El, lived upon his own mountain, called Mount Zaphon.

Much like the Greek pantheon led by Zeus on top of Mount Olympus, the Canaanite gods were larger than life. "They travel by giant strides— 'a thousand fields, ten thousand acres at each step'—and their control over human destiny is absolute. They are personifications of realities beyond human understanding and control." [7] On the other hand, the gods often acted humanly, and they displayed the same desires, faults, and actions as mankind. So, for example, in the Baal Cycle the gods are pictured as sitting down to eat at a banquet on top of El's mountain:

> There the gods had sat down to eat,
> The holy ones to a meal;
> Baal was standing by El.

The god El himself is portrayed as a bearded, sagely patriarchal figure, although in at least one text his attitude and behavior at a drinking feast were hardly stellar. Thus, it may rightly be argued that the Canaanite gods were made in the image of mankind.

Ugarit and Israel

Prior to the discovery of the Ugaritic tablets, little was known of ancient Canaan from extrabiblical literature. The Bible, of course, contains many

---

[6] Ibid., 130.
[7] Coogan, *Stories from Ancient Canaan*, 14.

references to Canaanite culture and, in particular, its religion. Most of these references, as would be expected, are negative and hostile toward the Canaanites. The Ugaritic texts, on the other hand, provide a primary, independent, and extensive witness to the beliefs of the Canaanites through a different lens. It is also important to note that the histories of Ugarit and Israel were broadly contemporary: Ugarit was at its politico-socio-economic zenith in the fifteenth–thirteenth centuries BC, and this was the period when Israel first entered the land of Canaan and began its time of nationhood.

Parallels between biblical literature and Ugaritic literature are vast, and they occur on various syntactical levels. We will not take time to review these parallels because they are commonly cited in the available literature.[8] The parallels are particularly striking in the poetical genre. For example, one of the defining features of Hebrew poetry is the device of parallelism; Ugaritic poetry also employs it as a dominant feature.

It is often claimed by modern scholars that biblical literature freely borrows from Canaanite literature. Mitchell Dahood's work, referenced above, strongly portrays the Hebrew psalms as greatly dependent on previous Canaanite texts and ideas. Where he goes too far is that he appears to suggest that biblical psalms are Canaanite psalms. But again, is that the only way to explain the nature of the relationship? Are the Hebrew writers crass plagiarists when they cite Canaanite material? Do they merely imitate and borrow the writings of the Canaanites and then apply them to their own cultural context? Here we will consider a few parallels to see one way in which the Hebrew writers may have been using Canaanite literature.

PSALM 29

Dahood argues that this hymn was an originally Canaanite product that was adapted by the Israelites for their own worship. He says,

> The recognition that this psalm is a Yahwistic adaption of an older Canaanite hymn to the storm-god Baal is . . . corroborated by the subsequent

---

[8] See, in particular, Mitchell Dahood, *Psalms*, vols. 1–3, Anchor Bible (Garden City, NY: Doubleday, 1966–1970). Admittedly, Dahood goes overboard in citation of parallels, yet much of his work is quite good.

discovery of tablets at Ras Shamra and by progress in the interpretation of these texts. Virtually every word in the psalm can now be duplicated in older Canaanite texts.[9]

Many scholars are in agreement with this explanation.[10] For certain, the vocabulary, meter, and structure of Psalm 29 have strong parallels in Ugaritic literature. Specific expressions in the psalm have clear and distinct correspondences with Canaanite phraseology. For example, the first verse of Psalm 29 says, "Ascribe to Yahweh, O heavenly beings, ascribe to Yahweh glory and strength." In Hebrew the term "heavenly beings" is literally translated as "the sons of god" (*bny 'elim*). In Canaanite mythology there is a group called the *bn ilm*, "the sons of El," and this epithet refers to the minor gods of the Canaanite pantheon of which El is the chief deity. Dahood's conclusion is a common one: "In the Old Testament the term was demythologized and came to refer to the angels or spiritual beings who are members of Yahweh's court and do his bidding." [11] The argument is clear-cut: the Hebrew psalmist simply borrowed this Canaanite expression, demythologized it, and then applied it to the religion of Yahweh.

Another example of a "borrowed" expression occurs in the repetitive phrase of Psalm 29 that refers to "the voice of Yahweh" (vv. 3, 4a, 4b, 5, 7, 8, 9). *Qol Yahweh* is employed throughout this psalm to denote the very power of Yahweh that is symbolized in thunder and lightning, and in other manifestations of a storm. Similar expressions are used throughout Canaanite literature to refer to Baal's power being personified in the rain and thunder; the storm is an indicator of the theophanic presence of Baal.

In fact, the entire psalm may be defined as one of storm imagery in order to depict the very presence of Yahweh on the earth. He is enthroned over all creation (v. 10), but he is yet immanent in the workings of the earth. This dominant storm imagery of Psalm 29 has strong and striking

---

[9] Ibid., 175.
[10] This interpretation was first presented by Harold L. Ginsburg, "A Phoenician Hymn in the Psalter," *XIX Congresso Internzionale degli Orientalisti* (Rome, 1935), 472–476; cf. T. H. Gaster, "Psalm 29," *Jewish Quarterly Review* 37 (1946–1947): 55–65; and Frank M. Cross, "Notes on a Canaanite Psalm in the Old Testament," *Bulletin of the American Schools of Oriental Research* 117 (1950): 19–21.
[11] Dahood, *Psalms*, vol. 1, 175.

parallels with the Baal imagery of the Ugaritic mythology—Baal was, in fact, the storm-god!

How are we to understand the many and significant parallels between Psalm 29 and Ugaritic literature? Again, many scholars merely see Psalm 29 as borrowed and sanitized Canaanite hymnody. In reality, it is more likely a polemic against Baal and Canaanite religion. The point of the psalm is the exaltation of Yahweh, and that glory is to be ascribed to his name and to none other. It is the name Yahweh that dominates this hymn; Yahweh is the *leitwort* ("leading word") of the song, appearing 18 times in a mere 11 verses! The Hebrew psalmist is a zealous monotheist, and this monotheism is at the expense of the Canaanite pantheon. Thus, it is not Baal who thunders, but "the God of glory thunders" (v. 3). And the "sons of El" ascribe glory to Yahweh and not to the chief deity of the Canaanites. This psalm is about the glory of Yahweh and of no other—the biblical writer's radical monotheism shines forth brightly through this polemic that taunts the false gods of Canaan.

THE GOD OF THE MOUNTAIN

Throughout the Old Testament the God of the Hebrews is associated with a mountain. The first mountain he is related to in Scripture is Mount Sinai/ Horeb, where Yahweh reveals himself to Moses and later gives Israel the law.[12] We read in Exodus 19:16–18 that

> On the morning of the third day there were thunders and lightnings and a thick cloud on the mountain and a very loud trumpet blast, so that all the people in the camp trembled. Then Moses brought the people out of the camp to meet God, and they took their stand at the foot of the mountain. Now Mount Sinai was wrapped in smoke because the LORD had descended on it in fire. The smoke of it went up like the smoke of a kiln, and the whole mountain trembled greatly.

A similar picture is given in 1 Kings 19, when the prophet Elijah travels to Horeb to meet with Yahweh (v. 8). And the Lord spoke to him:

---

[12] Some have attempted to argue that Horeb is not Mount Sinai but is another mountain in the same area. Others believe it may refer to the entire mountain range of which Mount Sinai is a part. It is, however, most likely that it is simply an alternate name for Mount Sinai and is used interchangeably with it (see, e.g., Ex. 3:12).

"Go out and stand on the mount before the LORD." And behold, the LORD
passed by, and a great and strong wind tore the mountains and broke in
pieces the rocks before the LORD. (v. 11)

The mountain of Sinai/Horeb is often referred to as "the mountain of God"
(Ex. 3:1; 4:27; 18:5; 24:13; 1 Kings 19:8), and at least one time as "the
mount of Yahweh" (Num. 10:33). This is the place where God dwells and
appears in theophany to his people.

Exodus 15:17 anticipates that another mountain will one day become
central to the worship of God, and he will dwell there with his people:

You will bring them in and plant them on your own mountain, the place,
O LORD, which you have made for your abode, the sanctuary, O Lord,
which your hands have established.

The passage looks ahead to the time when Israel will be established in
the land of promise, and Mount Zion in Jerusalem will be the center of
worship of Yahweh. Mount Zion is called "his holy mountain" (Ps. 48:1),
and the place where Yahweh "sits enthroned" (Ps. 9:11) and "dwells" (Isa.
8:18; Joel 3:17).

One of the early names in the Bible for the God of the Hebrews is *El
Shaddai*. In the context of God delivering the Hebrews out of Egypt, God
told Moses, "I appeared to Abraham, to Isaac, and to Jacob, as *El Shaddai*, but by my name Yahweh I did not make myself known to them" (Ex.
6:3, AT). Although often translated "God Almighty," it more likely means
"God of the mountain." [13]

As mentioned previously in this chapter, the head of the Canaanite
pantheon was El, who resided in a tent on a mountain, and from the mountain fresh waters flowed to all the earth. In addition, it was on this mountain
that the assembly of the gods met. The El names, such as El Shaddai, in
early Israelite literature led Frank Moore Cross to conclude that Yahweh
was originally an El figure.[14] As a god, however, he later shed many of the
characteristics of El and developed a separate identity.

---

[13] William F. Albright, "The Names *Shaddai* and *Abram*," *Journal of Biblical Literature* 54 (1935): 173–204.
[14] Frank M. Cross, *Canaanite Myth and Hebrew Epic: Essays in the History of the Religion of Israel* (Cambridge, MA: Harvard University Press, 1997 ed.).

Other scholars argue that perhaps Yahweh was originally a Baal figure, that is, a storm-god who revealed himself on a mountain in the theophany of a tempest. The appearance of Baal is described as follows:

Then Baal opened a slit in the clouds,
Baal sounded his holy voice,
Baal thundered from his lips . . .
The earth's high places shook.[15]

Yahweh is described in early Israelite literature with similar imagery; for example, in the Song of Deborah we read:

Yahweh, when you went out from Seir,
    when you marched from the region of Edom,
the earth trembled
    and the heavens dropped,
    yes, the clouds dropped water.
The mountains quaked before Yahweh,
    even Sinai before Yahweh, the God of Israel. (Judg. 5:4–5)

Some commentators believe that a process of syncretism occurred in which characteristics of both El and Baal blended and evolved into the deity Yahweh. Yahweh, then, was a sort of compilation of Canaanite gods who over time developed a singular, individual character.

The question is, of course, does this evolutionary, syncretistic understanding of the origin of Yahweh truly fit the evidence? Is Yahweh really a mere mutation of the Canaanite gods El and Baal? Are there not other ways to explain the many parallels? I have tried repeatedly in this book to demonstrate that the concept of polemical theology can be a fruitful approach to help interpret the parallels properly. It proves again to be helpful in the present context of the relationship between Israel and Ugarit.

An interesting polemical example of the motif of "the god of the mountain" appears in Isaiah 14:3–21. That passage consists primarily of an Israelite taunt against the king of Babylon. Part of the mockery is recorded as follows:

---

[15] Coogan, *Stories from Ancient Canaan*, 21.

How you are fallen from heaven,
    O Day Star, son of Dawn!
How you are cut down to the ground,
    you who laid the nations low!
You said in your heart,
    "I will ascend to heaven;
above the stars of God [El]
    I will set my throne on high;
I will sit on the mount of assembly
    in the far reaches of the north." (vv. 12–13)

The biblical writer scoffs at the king of Babylon by employing Canaanite mythology. He says that the Babylonian king desires to be like the Canaanite god El by having his throne on the "mount of assembly" which lies to the "north." But the reality is that the monarch of Babylon cannot even reach those heights. The truth is,

But you are brought down to Sheol,
    to the far reaches of the pit.
Those who see you will stare at you
    and ponder over you:
"Is this the man who made earth tremble,
    who shook kingdoms?" (vv. 15–16)

A more direct Israelite polemic against Canaanite mythology appears in Psalm 82. The psalm begins with the following literal translation:

God [Elohim] is taking his stand in the assembly of El,
    in the midst of the gods he [Elohim] will bring judgment. (v. 1)

This reference to Canaanite literature, in particular the meeting of the gathered council of gods before El, is not indicative of the God of Israel being part of the Canaanite pantheon. Rather, it is employed to picture the God of Israel as assaulting the pagan pantheon, or as Dahood comments, it is "where God passes judgment on the pagan deities." [16] Here is seething hostility by the psalmist against Canaanite theology, as he claims instead

---

[16] Dahood, *Psalms*, vol. 2, 268.

that the one true God has deposed the pagan gods and that he is the only ruler of the earth (v. 8). This particular polemic is a common one in the Psalms (cf. Ps. 29:1–2 and 89:6–9).

Polemical theology certainly does not answer every question about the relationship of the Old Testament to ancient Near Eastern literature and life. There is much to that relationship that simply cannot be understood and explained by the use of polemics. At times, however, polemical theology can serve as a solid and reliable interpretive lens by which one can properly see the significance of a parallel. In addition, and of utmost importance, is the truth that the biblical writers often employed polemical theology as an instrument to underscore the uniqueness of the Hebrew worldview in contrast to other ancient Near Eastern conceptions of the universe and how it operates. In this day and age, when a considerable number of scholars seek to diminish the originality and uniqueness of the Old Testament, this is no small thing.

General Index

Aaron, 28–29; confrontation of with Pharaoh's magicians, 45, 117, 118n30
Abraham, 20
Ahab, 29, 30, 103
Ahmosis (son of Ah), 82
Akhenaten, 115
Akkadians/Akkadian empire, 44, 76
Amenemhet I, 90, 91
Ammisaduqa, 50
Amon-Re, hymn to, 106–107, 127–128
Anath, 58–59. *See also* Baal-Anath myth
Ancient Near Eastern studies, 1; beginnings of research in, 12–16; impact of the discovery of cuneiform archives on, 19–21
'Andjety, 115
Andrews, C. A. R., 14
Anu, 62, 72
Anubis, 67–70, 67n6
Apsu, 36, 37, 43
archaeology, in the Near East: excavations of the Hittite city of Bogazkoy (Hattusa), 19; modern period of (1945–present), 21–23; in the nineteenth century, 13—16; pre-nineteenth century archaeology, 12–13. *See also* Egypt, excavations in; Mesopotamia, excavations in
Asherah (Astarte), 71, 103
Ashertu, 71–72
Ashurbanipal, 54
Assyria/Assyrians, 15, 44
Atrahasis. *See* flood accounts, and the Epic of Atrahasis

Atum, 27, 42, 56, 99n5, 114
autobiography: "fictional autobiography," 77; "pseudo-autobiography," 77

Baal, 28, 30–31, 44, 58–59, 133, 134, 137, 139; Isaiah's criticism of, 108; power of, 136
Baal Cycle, 133, 134
Baal-Anath myth, 133–134
Babel und Bibel (Delitzsch), 33
Babylon/Babylonians, 15, 44; taunting of the king of Babylon, 139–140
Bata, 67–70, 67n6
Bauefre, 123, 124
Bel, 53
Bes, 103
Bible, the: modernist views of biblical history, 22–23; and Near Eastern creation accounts, 17–18. *See also* creation accounts, of Genesis and the Near Eastern texts; Ugaritic literature, parallels with biblical literature
Bilgames, death of, 49–50
Birch, Samuel, 15–16
birth stories, 75–76; Hittite birth stories, 83–84; and the Legend of Sargon, 76–79; of Moses, 78–79; and the Myth of Horus (the "exposed-infant motif"), 79–83, 86–87; parallels between the birth story of Moses and of Horus, 81–83; the use of polemic in, 86–87. *See also* persecuted child motif, analysis of
Bogazkoy (Hattusa), 19
Book of the Dead, 56

ex nihilo (Latin: "out of nothing"), 42, 43

"exile-return" motif, 93–95

Fecht, Gerhard, 100, 107, 109

flood accounts, 47–48; Assyrian flood account, 16–18; Berossos's account, 53–54; and the "Death of Bilgames" account, 49–50; Egyptian flood account, 55–57; and the Epic of Atrahasis, 50–52, 53, 57, 59, 62; and the Epic of Gilgamesh, 52–53, 54–55, 57, 59, 62; Hebrew flood account, 17; Sumerian flood account, 48–49; the use of polemic in, 61–63. *See also* flood accounts, differences between the Genesis and Near Eastern accounts

flood accounts, differences between the Genesis and Near Eastern accounts, 57–61; approaches of to morality, 57–58; and the concept of covenant, 58; differences in specific details, 59; genre differences, 58–59; theological differences, 57

Frankfort, Henri, 116

Gardiner, Alan, 107

Genesis, book of: demythologization in, 34–35; as "exalted prose narrative," 44; as a "gentle polemic," 31n15; and the Marduk myth, 33. *See also* creation accounts, of Genesis and the Near Eastern texts

Gilgamesh. *See* flood accounts, and the Epic of Gilgamesh; "spurned seductress" motif, and the Epic of Gilgamesh

God, 46, 85, 86, 121, 140, 141; "I Am That I Am" name of, 100–101, 100–101n10, 105–109; as a jealous God, 73; reasons of for the deliverance of Israel from Egypt, 127; sovereignty of, 41, 45. *See also* Yahweh (Hebrew: *yhwh*)

gods, Near Eastern: creation of, 40–41; creative work of, 43

Grayson, Albert, 77

"Great Hymn to Khnum, The," 38–39

"Great Wild Bull Is Lying Down." *See* "Death of Bilgames, The"

Gunkel, Hermann, 25–26, 33

Hamath, 105

Haran, 20

Hardedef, 123

Harsiese, 115

Hathor, 99, 113, 115

Hatti, 75

Hattusa, 83, 84

Hays, Harold, 124

Heidel, Alexander, 17, 37, 45

Hengstenberg, Ernst W., 29, 117

Herculaneum, 12–13

Herodotus, 12; goals of, 12

hieroglyphs, 14–15

Hirah, 65

Hittites, 36, 71, 73, 84

Hoffmeier, James, 26, 72–73, 79, 86n25

Horemhab, 115

Hornung, Erik, 100, 107, 109

Humbaba, 72

Hunt, Joel, 133

Hurrians, 20, 36

Huwawa, 50

"I am that I am" statements, 100–101, 100–101n10; understanding the meaning of, 105–109. *See also* Yahweh (Hebrew: *yhwh*), extrabiblical references to

Ilimilku, 133

imago Dei (Latin: "image of God"), 42

Irvin, Dorothy, 72, 73

Isaac, 20, 138

Isaiah, taunting of Baal by, 108

Ishtar, 72, 77, 78, 83

Isis, 116n25; Isis-Horus relationship, 80–81

Scripture Index